Best wishes

[signature]

Days We'll Remember All Our Lives

Steve Little

authorHOUSE®

AuthorHouse™
1663 Liberty Drive
Bloomington, IN 47403
www.authorhouse.com
Phone: 1-800-839-8640

© 2010 Steve Little. All rights reserved.

No part of this book may be reproduced, stored in a retrieval system, or transmitted by any means without the written permission of the author.

First published by AuthorHouse 11/11/2010

ISBN: 978-1-4520-5678-4 (sc)

Printed in the United States of America

This book is printed on acid-free paper.

Because of the dynamic nature of the Internet, any Web addresses or links contained in this book may have changed since publication and may no longer be valid. The views expressed in this work are solely those of the author and do not necessarily reflect the views of the publisher, and the publisher hereby disclaims any responsibility for them

By the same author

MORE THAN JUST A LIFE
(a thrilling World War One Drama)

Daily Mail - it impressed us with its plotting and its energy.

Howard Swan - Touching …sensitive … emotional… thoughtful … immensely moving …personal … enthralling …gripping …sad …pathetic …ghastly in its detail … critical of the awfulness of the establishment …a tremendous insight into a mind disturbed … quite, quite excellent.

Mr Chiesman from Surrey - Nine out of ten – I like the twist in the tail!

Mr B Terry from Essex - I could not put it down and read it in a day – a great story!

For Chrissie, my wife, and for my children,
Andy and Jenny, their spouses
Helen and Ian, and the grandchildren,
Cameron and Abigail

CONTENTS

INTRODUCTION xi
1. "I'M IN NEXT AND I'M RAMAN SUBBA ROW" 1
2. "DO I REALLY HAVE TO WEAR A CAP UNTIL I'M 16?" 11
3. EARLY DAYS 18
4. WHAT'S IN A NAME? 25
5. THIS LATIN......IT'S ALL GREEK TO ME! 37
6. BOXING – IT'LL MAKE A MAN OF YOU SON! 41
7. "AND LASTLY EITHER A HAMMER OR A BRUSH AND DON'T KICK THE SHAVINGS OUT OF THE DOOR WHEN YOU LEAVE" 47
8. ART FOR ART'S SAKE? 55
9. YOU'RE IN THE ARMY NOW, LAD – WELL, AT LEAST FOR ONE DAY A WEEK! 60
10. THE WORST WEEK OF MY LIFE...? WELL, AT LEAST WE MISSED RONNIE BIGGS AND HIS MATES! 69
11. ONE STEP AHEAD! 96
12. COULD I HAVE THE SIGHTSCREEN MOVED PLEASE? 99
13. UNDER 15s ONLY 103
14. RAIN STOPPED PLAY! OR HAS IT? 114
15. CHEATS NEVER PROSPER, OR DO THEY!? 118
16. MAKE SURE YOU CONCENTRATE DURING FRENCH REPRODUCTION! 130
17. WHAT TIME IS THE LAST TRAIN TO CHELMSFORD? 137
18. "THIS IS THE ONLY WAY WE'LL EVER GET TO CAMBRIDGE! HOWEVER, WE COULD END UP AT THE OLD BAILEY!" 145
19. FROM A SNOWMAN TO A DOLPHIN! 153
20. "GET TREVOR BAILEY OUT OF THE BAR – THE GAME'S FINISHED!" 160
21. WHO WOULD LIKE TO BUY THESE TICK......? DAMN! 167
22. IT'S MY PARTY AND I'M DEFINITELY GOING TO HAVE MARILYN MONROE! 174
23. I REALLY WOULD LIKE TO LOOK LIKE ROGER MOORE 182
24. "AFTER THIS NEXT RECORD WE'LL ASK THE NEAREST GIRL TO US TO DANCE!" 189

25. "YOU KNOW WHAT? – THIS IS A MENTAL HOME!" 197
26. THE IMPORTANCE OF BEING THE HEAD BOY 205
27. WELCOME TO THE PREFECT'S ROOM! 209
28. I HEAR THE SOUNDS OF DISTANT DRUMS! 215
29. AN INCH MAKES ALL THE DIFFERENCE! 221
30. SCHOOLBOY PRANKS? – WELL IT SEEMED FUNNY AT THE TIME 230
31. HEALTH AND SAFETY? – IT'S NOT BEEN INVENTED YET! 236
32. GIRLS DON'T MAKE PASSES AT BOYS WEARING GLASSES .247
33. TRAGEDY! 252
34. YES – BUT YOU HAVEN'T GOT A FORD MUSTANG! 256
35. SOMETHING IN THE AIR 268
36. THE END OF THOSE DAYS 276

INTRODUCTION

They certainly were the days we'll remember all our lives. From the age of eleven until we completed our A-levels at eighteen, almost one hundred fresh faced boys, who joined King Edward VI Grammar School in Chelmsford in September 1960, experienced the highs and lows of secondary school life. Fresh from the success at scraping through the eleven plus examination, we joined over five hundred boys already at the school but there were no girls.

At the age of eleven the girls were just an irritation but within three years or so they were to become a necessity. The girls were not that far away with the all-girls High School a few hundred yards along the Broomfield road. A couple of miles further along that road there was the mixed Technical High School with about half the pupils young ladies. These were the three schools that those who had successfully passed the eleven-plus would attend. If you did not pass the exam or chose not to enter then there was a whole collection of mixed secondary schools dotted around the town.

Known as KEGS, the Grammar School had been founded in 1551 but replaced a school that had already been in existence for some years before. It had a fine record as a school in 1960 and it still does to this day.

The vibrant Old Chelmsfordians' Association (OCA) maintains a link to the school and provides something that many of the 1960 intake still use to keep in touch, just as boys from previous and subsequent years do. There are still active old boys in the OCA who were at the school in the 1930s and some even in the 1920s.

For those who joined in 1960 we were to experience the most potently changing times of the century. From the austere post war 40s and 50s we had the swinging 60s, or at least they were from about 1963. The Beatles' sound hit the world, we narrowly avoided nuclear war over the Cuban missile crisis, the birth pill arrived for the ladies and with D. H. Lawrence's Lady Chatterley's Lover being allowed to be published, the floodgates were opened for the free and easy society we have today.

School life changed with it. We were the early baby boomers born in 1948 and 1949 and were now moving towards our teenage years at the time when Harold Macmillan, the Prime Minister, famously told our parents' generation that "They had never had it so good!"

I do not believe that my parents thought this in 1960 when it was hard for them to meet the cost of me going to KEGS. In fact, there were a number of children who were not entered for the eleven-plus at the request of the parents as they could not afford the extra cost of the uniform, special clothing, equipment and so on.

By the time we had left the school in 1968 we were into the hippy and flower power age. The Beatles had pretty well come and gone. There was this thing called homosexuality that was never spoken about before but now became acceptable. National Service had gone. The Death Penalty had also gone. Girl's skirts had, thankfully, got very short but then there was a tinge of disappointment because the girls opting for the shortest skirts generally seemed to have the fattest legs!

Through all this, KEGS life carried on much as before but gradually even that became a little more permissive and one has to say a little ill disciplined. However, as with the boys who went before us, we did work hard and the school gave us all a great opportunity to make something of ourselves. Yet we did have some great fun both in and out of school. A whole group of us from that time remain firm friends to this day and some have even known each other for well over fifty years as we met at Primary School.

This book tells stories that are all true except where stated and are perhaps a little embellished over the years but they are all based on what occurred at the time and probably happened at schools all over the world and you will, of course, recall your own similar experiences. You should, therefore, have no problem relating to these.

My own two children tell me that their schooldays did not have such goings on but perhaps in fifty years time they might have their own stories to tell, as will the schoolchildren of today. The problem comes with trying to remember them all so I decided to put these down in writing before the old memory completely fades!

Some of the character's names have been changed to protect their virtue. I hope you can relate to the stories and that they bring back memories of those schooldays of long and not so long ago. They were not all that bad although they often seemed like they were at the time!

1

"I'M IN NEXT AND I'M RAMAN SUBBA ROW"

It's May 6th 1960; a warm if slightly overcast Friday. We have the day off from our primary school as the fragrant Princess Margaret was marrying this photographer chap called Anthony Armstrong-Jones. We were all given the day off so we could watch it on the telly but of course not a lot of people, at least in our street, actually had one. Radio was the preferred choice of entertainment for many. However, to we youngsters, popular entertainment was hard to find on the dial and we were only just getting into music. "Pick of the Pops" on a Sunday with "Fluff" Freeman was virtually the only popular music programme and he had just that week told us the Everly Brothers were number one with "Cathy's Clown".

With no TV and little interest in **listening** to a boring wedding, my friends and me had already made plans for the day. However, before that there was an event of more significance to this ten year old as it was the day when the 11-plus results came out. Along with my friends we would at least be at home when the postman came. Dad was at work at the factory as it was only the schoolchildren who had the day off. Mum was at home as she was not yet back working full time.

The letter dropped on the mat, in those days there was no junk mail to discard and there was just this one brown envelope with an official postage mark.

I was allowed to open it and there was one long paragraph. There was no "Pass" or "Fail" or "Yes" or "No". I read through the paragraph quickly hardly taking in what was there. I handed it back to Mum, as I was not sure whether it meant "Pass" or "Fail". Mum had to read it twice to make sure I had passed.

I think I was elated but in those days no one "did" elation or whooping and hollering – it was just a calm "oh good" and now I can get outside and organise the cricket. Dad would be home just after midday for his dinner (lunch had yet to be invented for the working classes) and whilst inwardly overjoyed would not effuse and rush out and buy me a new bike!

No one had a phone so I could not ring my friends to see how they got on. It was a sort of relief but no great deal for any of us. We went to the largest primary school, Kings Road, in the Chelmsford area and we were in the top class so I guess it was to be expected that we would pass but one could never be sure about these things.

As usual at about 10 in the morning our cricket gang began to assemble outside my house; the second house in a cul-de-sac of sixteen semi-detached council houses. The road was quiet with only a few houses owning a car and the men that drove them were at work and the cars were gone.

Terence "Kettles" Ketley lived just round the corner and he came round first. He was a teenager and already at the Grammar School. I hoped to join him there because like everyone else we selected King Edward V1 as our number one choice if we did pass the 11-plus. Whilst the pass was confirmed the school we would be attending in the September would be advised at a later date.

Gradually the cricket gang began to turn up on their bikes. Nigel "Otter" Ottley and Simon Hughes came first – they had got through then came Ian "Gus" Gunn – "Yes" he was there too. Rob the younger brother of "Kettles" arrived but at eight did not understand what we were talking about – we only tolerated one so young as he was cannon fodder for our fast off-breaks or similar in the street cricket match.

Neil Ritchie lived opposite me and he was nine – more cannon fodder. He was a northerner (well, from Leicester) and a bad loser, even worse than me! He often cried when he was out and went home but he would always slink back within the half hour.

So the Princess was to be ignored as we had the more serious job of starting our match in the road between number 4 and number 3 opposite. I lived at 4 and the front gate was made of vertical bars held in place with a top and bottom horizontal piece and one diagonal. It was about four feet high and we drew a chalk line across the three middle bars and this was the batting wicket; five yards away was a stump placed in the grass that edged the other side of the road.

Essex Avenue was a road made of concrete sections dropped in with thin tarmac joins between the sections, which were useful to form our two boundaries. The wall to my house and the Ritchie's at Number 3 were the other boundaries and the playing area was in total about twenty yards square. Only a tennis ball could be used and bowling was underarm. The strict rules were that you could hit boundaries but not too hard in case the ball did some damage to flowers in someone's garden or even break a window.

The first house in the road at about deep mid on was where the Cornwalls lived. Mr Cornwall was a postman. They had two daughters, Anne and Sandra who were about our age and if the ball went in their garden they did not mind us getting it back as long as we used the gate and the path. The house next to mine, number 2, was where the Brookers lived. Marion was about the same age as "Kettles" but we never ever saw her. Mr B had a posh car and we dreaded it being parked there, as it would be at short square leg and directly in our way. Thankfully he worked a lot so the car was only there in the evenings and weekends. If he was on holiday and at home, cricket would be delayed by "car stopped play" or we would adjourn to Rutland Road rec. and start another match but with overarm bowling and much bigger boundaries. If the ball went over the Brooker's we had to creep along on all fours past their windows to get it or use a replacement ball and collect the other one after dark.

Our matches were three or four a side but we played as Test teams so if I was in the England team I might be Raman Subba Row (England's star batsman of that summer), John Murray (wicketkeeper) and Fred Trueman (bowler). The other team might be Pakistan and we all delighted in being Imtiaz Ahmed, Saeed Mohammed or similar!

So our celebratory match gets underway. My bat, my ball and my pitch so at the fall of my team's first wicket I announce, "I'm in next and I'm Raman Subba Row" (the best batsman). "Kettles" always had us keeping a meticulous scorebook and promised to prepare our averages. He started the task but we never did see the completed statistics! Our games rarely reached a result because the next day the numbers and the personnel playing changed so we started another match.

Boys being boys, batsmen sometimes got carried away and hit out with big sixes. Neighbours' windows were never smashed but there was one incident of note. As our pitch was just in the first part of the Avenue there were houses in the next road not that far away, about fifty yards. The house on the corner whose gardens ran down to the side of the Cornwall's house was where the Mays lived. Chris "Whiff" May was our age but no sportsman and he had an older brother, Roger. "Whiff" got that name as he had the innate ability to fart at will, a talent the rest of us had yet to master. Their Dad was a policeman from the local sub office but he did not have our section of the estate as part of his beat but was always someone not to cross and to treat with respect. This particular day he was up a ladder cleaning the upstairs' back windows. One of our number got carried away and hit a mighty six over cow corner, a shot not allowed in our local rules and definitely a "six and out" situation.

The tennis ball soared onwards and upwards and struck PC May squarely on his bottom. He dropped his leather and had to hold on to the ladder to make sure he did not fall off it. It took him several seconds to get his balance. In high dudgeon he looked back at where moments before we had been happily playing – the whole street was deserted! We had all perfected the art of diving behind low walls, into flowerbeds or behind side gates when these emergencies occurred.

Play was suspended whilst PC May completed the windows and eventually took down his ladder. I would have to ask "Whiff" to get my ball for me later in the day.

So this momentous day came to an end. The Princess and the photographer sailed off into the sunset and into a marriage destined not to last. That was not the end of the cricket for that summer. Once school broke up for the holidays we started on our more serious cricket sessions. Worried that we were now outgrowing playing in the street and not wishing to cause more damage to the gardens or even be responsible for a possible fall from a ladder, we all moved our cricket pitch to the recreation ground on another part of the estate.

The Rutland Road rec. was an area of grass set in the middle of houses that bordered it on each of its four sides. However, it was at the back of the houses. Its size was about that of half a normal football pitch and it had four swings in one corner – one entrance to it was for the gang-mowers and the other was a narrow footpath between two of the houses.

It was nicely contained with a six feet tall wire fence all around protecting the back gardens of the neat houses.

In the winter this had been our football pitch where we played diagonally across it using a Frido plastic ball and either our jumpers and coats, or a cricket stump, for each goalpost.

For the cricket we still split into England versus another country and played maybe as many as three different roles just as we had done in the street cricket. "Kettles" continued to keep the scores and the matches often continued, as before, into subsequent days. We used a tennis ball and proper cricket bats with the usual set of stumps. "Kettles" had a Denis Compton signed bat that had seen better days and another lad had one signed by Len Hutton. The fact that these two great cricketers were long since retired the bats had really seen better days!

The tennis ball was easy to spin off the hard "wicket" (the bumpy centre circle of the football pitch!) yet equally easy to hit but, being softer than a cricket ball, it was relatively comfortable to catch especially for the young Ketley and Ritchie and, should it go over the fences, would not damage the plants in the surrounding gardens.

I was always keen to be wicketkeeper and despite the soft ball I "borrowed" my Dad's creosoting gloves as they looked a little like wicket keeping gloves. All they really did was make my hands smell of creosote for several days after wearing them despite repeated washing.

I was still always Raman Subba Row in the matches but I am not sure my performances matched those of my hero against the South Africans that summer.

Occasionally the big hitters would clear the fence although this was strictly against the rules and would definitely mean the batsman would be declared "out".

On one day the ball cleared the fence. Over time we got to know those residents that were friendly towards us getting the ball and those who were not. For some gardens it had to be a case of lost ball, as we knew we would get told to go away in no uncertain terms if we knocked on that particular door to ask for our ball back. Sometimes we recklessly did climb over the fence into any one of these gardens in the hope that the less than friendly owner might be out.

On such occasions, we always sent one of our younger brothers over the fence first of all mainly because we did not want to get caught ourselves and secondly it was easy to browbeat the younger one into doing it! Also, if caught the owner might be more sympathetic to a little 8 year old!

So on this occasion Timmy Hughes, younger brother of Simon, was helped over the fence. Crouching low he moved across the garden towards our ball. Unfortunately for him, the owner, it turned out, was unexpectedly at home and walked into the garden with some vegetables to plant. Timmy froze and looked pleadingly at his older brother. Simon pointed to the tree to Timmy's right and pointed upwards. Timmy got the message and like a rat up a drainpipe was ensconced and hidden in the lower branches before the neighbour noticed.

We returned to our cricket with a replacement ball and left Timmy to his fate. An hour later he was still there because the owner had bought a lot of plants and was taking time to get them into the ground just as he wanted.

Eventually Timmy was able to get down, pick up the ball and climb back over the fence at which time the poor lad broke down into tears. He was given short shrift by his brother and told to go and field on the boundary.

August drew to a close after we had all taken a week or two away with our parents on holiday. Those from the cricket matches throughout that summer who had now reached aged 11 joined the rest of the boys from Kings Road School and "Kettles" at the Grammar School. In fact of the one hundred boys who joined the first year in September 1960 the old Kings Road pupils accounted for fourteen – Otter, Simon, Gus, Froggy Frost, Steve Robbins, Lawrence Hatchard, John Denton, John Tingey, David Fenton, Ian Robinson (later Brown), Clive Haworth, Phil Mason, Graham King and me.

We did not know it at the time but the 11-plus was something of a watershed and got us to one of the country's best schools both then and now in terms of its academic performance. Some like me found it hard going in the early years, some even hated it but most enjoyed it. What has been good to hear as we now enter middle age is that many of our Kings Road contemporaries who did not enter or did not pass the 11-plus have done just as well for themselves.

As September arrived we geared ourselves for the culture shock that was to be our first term at big school

2

"DO I REALLY HAVE TO WEAR A CAP UNTIL I'M 16?"

The euphoria the parents felt when their son passed his eleven-plus exam and got a place at the Grammar School soon dissipated when the reality of the costs involved became apparent.

"How much!" my Dad said when my Mum showed him the receipt from Bond's, the high street retailer in Chelmsford who stocked all you needed to kit your son out for his new school from that autumn.

"£29, that's nearly two weeks wages and I bet there's more to pay out yet?"

Steve Little

"Not too much," said Mum, lying.

Mum and Dad had received a letter from the school informing them of the required uniform and other items of clothing needed for other activities. Everything had to be labelled. So "Stephen Little" appeared on everything. How I hated that! "Mum," I said, "I wanted Steve, I hate Stephen!"

"Oh shush your noise," was the only response I got.

The basic uniform was cap, a choice of two grey thick shirts that made you itch, tie (black with two thin red stripes every inch or so), pair of short trousers (only the tall boys like Garwood and Milton had long trousers in the first year – by the second year all of us but Kiddie were in long ones!), two pairs of long knee-length grey socks with red and black hoops at the top and of course the resplendent school blazer.

This was essentially black with a round school badge on the breast pocket. The lapels and collars had a red braid all the way round. All boys wore this up until the end of the third year then the braid could be taken off, which normally meant parents having to buy a new blazer. The less well off would have the braid removed by Mum but underneath the black colour was much darker than the rest of the blazer, so the dual black effect in the fourth year was an indication of hard-up parents finding it difficult to pay out for a new blazer. It was always a little embarrassing for their child.

Black shoes with laces were required. A satchel for our books was not something we had at Primary School so this was also needed. Fortunately with my birthday being in June it meant grandparents and aunts and uncles could buy this sort of thing plus pencil cases, protractors, rubbers, pens etc thus saving some cost to my parents.

A gabardine black mac would be needed for the winter and would be something to be acquired at the end of October when finances had been replenished.

The basic sport's clothing was a red and black school football shirt with two buttons in the neck and a pair of dark blue, serge shorts the seams of which forever rubbed on our thighs and made them chapped and sore. Socks were black with two red rings at the top. For PE we needed a plain white tee shirt and white shorts and socks plus black plimsolls. Not for us designer trainers or tracksuits and sweat tops or replica football shirts.

Woodwork lessons were given high importance at school for some reason as if, like Latin, it was needed at O-level if you wanted to go to Oxbridge! We had to have a specific apron (and that was fair enough) to protect our school clothes. To it Mum sewed on the "Stephen Little" tag and then we had to add our form number "1B" and then our set number, "3" in my case (the 100 boys having been split into 4 sets of 25 in alphabetical order).

So with all this equipment to buy, my parents had to forego a proper holiday in 1960 and we went out for "days" to save money –if you ever told friends that you were going out for days for your holiday it was yet another social embarrassment to cope with as it again indicated that your parents had little money! Fortunately most of my friends were in the same boat.

As first years we were aghast to discover that we had to wear our caps until we sat our O-levels when we were 15 or 16. In 1960 the common hairstyle was "short back and sides" unless your parents could afford the extra sixpence for a "Perry Como" or a "Boston" but as the sixties wore on the Beatles arrived and invented long hair only previously sported by beatniks or other freaks! So as we neared 16 our hair got longer and the cap, which none us wished to wear anyway, was then normally perched precariously on the back of the head.

Most of us were frightened stiff to go home from school or about the town without our cap whilst we were in school uniform in case we were spotted by a Prefect or a Master. I had to pass the house of Gaffney, a Full Prefect, so did not dare act in anyway to draw his wrath when I passed by on my bike. Just up from him there was a disagreeable lad who was a lot older than me who had a downer on anyone from a "posh" school and always tried to accost me as I rode by and tried to steal my cap. As it was near Gaffney's I did not feel comfortable taking it off so had to run the gauntlet. In the end I had to change my route but this took me past Nicholson's house and then Ketley's both of whom became Prefects so again no stuffing the cap in my pocket!

For we cricketers the cap had another use even if we were only playing in the park during the school holidays. If my hero Raman or Ted Dexter and Colin Cowdrey wore them at the crease and in the field then so would we!

By the time we were 14 or 15 we started showing an interest in girls. The cap was hardly "cool" as the youngsters say today and a definite obstruction to creating a desirable image. Fortunately the Girls' High School up the road from us insisted their pupils wore berets and bonnets so we did not feel out of place when chatting them up but the other schoolgirls were less accommodating and often thought we were stuck up "grammar" boys. The cap was a sort of social stigma and one we all disliked. As soon as we left the school the rules changed so third and fourth years were excused the cap – nowadays however … what's a cap?!

Occasionally boys would lose their caps by being accosted by a yob like the one I had on our estate or we might leave them on buses or trains. One day one of our number had his cap tossed into the gang mower as it cut the sport's field and it was shredded into hundreds of little pieces, after it had been taken by another boy and thrown there as a joke! Not wanting to have the embarrassment of explaining this to parents in such circumstances we would simply pinch one from a first year who was in no position to retaliate!

When the long haul through to the sixth form ended we were released from some of the strict uniform code. No caps and a different tie with a sort of orangey-red and yellow thick stripe. We could move away from the grey thick shirts and onto thinner white ones. Brown shoes were now permitted and most of us switched to them because it was something different to the majority of the boys. The brown shoes hardly went with grey trousers and black blazer but, never mind, we were sixth formers and the shackles were off at last!

If you became a sub prefect you wore yet another different tie but this time it was given to you by the school so it saved our parents yet more cost. The tie was a rather nifty one with a red, black and white thin stripe that was even passable to wear to your older cousins' weddings, events that seemed like a weekly occurrence at that time of our lives! Full prefects were even better off with an elegant black tie with a thin green, yellow, even thinner blue denoting their illustrious and lofty position in the school as one of only about ten. This tie was also that of the Old Boys, the Old Chelmsfordians, so those prefects could all use them for a few years afterwards at the Old Boys' dinners.

Sadly, many of we boys have kept memorabilia including, in some cases, these ties. Many of us still have our school reports, which do make interesting reading. I even have a cricket "box" which has the inscription "KEGS 2nd XI" inked inside it – I found it only recently and not wishing to be accused of stealing thought I might return it but then thought better of it – I might donate it to science to see how many DNA strands it contains!

3

EARLY DAYS

We all turned up in early September for our first day resplendent in our brand new uniforms including that obligatory cap! With my friend "Kettles" already at the school and living close to me, I was invited to walk with him and another boy, Roger Bird, and they took me along on that first morning. Also being with those Kings Road Primary boys, the new school was not so daunting as for others from the smaller schools that had to come along on their own. On the walk to school we whistled along to "Apache" by the Shadows that "Fluff" Freeman told us was this week's Number One!

On that first day, the new boys all stood in a great long line in the playground and our names were called out in strict alphabetical order so Form 1A was all those boys from Ankers to Fitzgerald, 1B was Forster to Moon and 1C Mottram to Wood. 1A were told they would be based at the main school but 1B and 1C along with 2A and 2B would be housed each day, for at least every morning and part of some afternoons, at the old Friars School in Friars Place Chelmsford, situated near what is now the County Cricket Ground.

There was quite a contrast in size between the rows of boys standing in the playground. Some were nearly 12 and some were only just 11 so there was in some cases a lot of difference in physique. Some of the bigger boys actually wore long trousers but the majority wore short ones. One poor boy had not yet received his blazer from Bond's the outfitters and had to wear his mackintosh on what was a very warm and dry day!

1B and 1C trooped off in a crocodile through the town to Friars. At lunchtime we all trooped back to the school again and did this most days but sometimes we stayed at Friars for afternoon lessons in our individual classes but we spent at least part of every afternoon at the main school for certain lesson periods such as double period Games, Woodwork, Art etc.

I never did have school dinners choosing instead to go to my grandparents nearby throughout my time at the school. I felt I missed out on quite a bit by doing this especially the games of cricket and football on the playing field next to the school but at least I escaped the attentions of the boys from the second and third years who would initiate the first years by throwing them into one of the several prickly holly bushes in the school grounds!

Compared with Primary School the teachers were very intimidating. Most wore their flowing gowns and addressed us only by our surnames or simply as "boy". This was quite a change from the softer, mainly lady, teachers we had at our Primary Schools.

In our early days we were given a copy of the "School Rules" and were supervised whilst we read them thoroughly. We got to know them quite well as the teachers and prefects often made us write out in our own hand a copy of the rules instead of the more traditional "lines" as a form of punishment. "Detention" for serious "offences" still took place on Saturday mornings but this was soon phased out. We had what was called "Checks" which would mean staying behind after school in one of the classrooms, supervised by a prefect, this was meant to be for "offences" such as running along the corridors or not wearing your cap outside the school grounds.

The school had two grass compounds inside the main building with arched walkways around all four sides. For very minor "offences" the prefects would make us stand around the outside between the arches for anything up to an hour after school before they came and told us we could leave. On more than one occasion the prefect would forget about us and go home so we were there for a lot longer!

Of course, in those days no parent ever picked us up from the school for which we were glad, as it would have been so embarrassing if they did.

At break time in the morning we had a bottle of milk but not for me as I can only drink it if it's in something! However, I used to exchange mine with a friend for an iced bun from the tuck shop so it was not all that bad.

There was not one obese child that I can recall in our year but there were some big lads that could give us a hard time. I see some of them now and they don't look half so threatening now that they are granddads!

Mr Fanshawe had joined as Head in 1949, the year that many of the 1960 intake were born and unbelievably he is still alive and living in Frinton-on-sea in Essex and now approaching his century.

For the new boys the prefects were the bane of our lives. The senior, or "full" as they were called, prefects were not so bad and seemed as if at 18 they were as old as our Dads. I still see some of then today at the Old Chelmsfordians' Association (OCA) and they don't seem to have changed! The sub prefects were the ones that dished out the discipline and were the least popular.

Some teachers were friendly but most were less so.

School representative sports were not really available to us until the second year as the youngest team was Under 13s but we did have a weekly dose of "Games" for a double period of 80 minutes. This would include football up to Christmas, hockey after Christmas and cricket in the summer term. The dreaded cross-country run was the bane of our sporting lives though. All hundred or so of us would leave the school gates into Broomfield Road and turn left and then left into Westfield Avenue. From there we would go into Maltese Road and then through what was called "The Gardens" and out into Swiss Avenue and then left into Park Avenue and then we would cross Roxwell Road and have a breather at the large oak tree at the top of Admiral's Park. This was about two miles!

It would take all of five minutes for the crocodile of runners to catch up with the hares at the front with the tortoises panting at the rear. From the top of Admiral's we would run down to the bridge. Go across to the fields and then cut back to Waterhouse Lane near the fire station. From there we would head up that road and into Cedar Avenue and back to the school. That was another two miles making four miles in all.

It was one of the greatest culture shocks to then have to strip off and go into the communal showers. No one apart from our Mums and Dads had seen us at this age with our clothes off. Of course, we had not yet become "men" and it was a fright if we saw what we might become when we shared the shower with the fifth formers on occasions! One of the Sports Masters, Mr Elder, would also run the four miles with us and join us in the shower not only did he have hair where the fifth formers had theirs but he had it all over his body and he had a member more developed than anyone else, it was most off putting for an 11 year old!

Talking of "Houses" the entire 1960 intake were assigned to one of the four "Houses" – Strutt, Tindal, Holland or Mildmay. If your father or older brother had been to the school before you then you would be given their house. If you were a boarder you were always put into Tindal. The houses were named after famous people from Chelmsford.

I recall sitting in 1B during our first few days all in our neat rows of desks and all in alphabetical order. Now Strutt was the house to be in as they had been "Cock House" for the previous few years. You did not want to be in Mildmay as they were the traditional "woodenspoonists". Either of the other two would just about be acceptable.

Our form master went round the class starting alphabetically with Forster. My friend Simon Hughes I knew would be in Holland like his father before him. Another friend Clive Haworth got Strutt – the lucky fellow. Ian Gunn looked at me dismayed when he got Mildmay but brightened up when I got the same.

Still none of this did us any harm. Simon and Ian, a Mildmay House Captain when in the 6th form, became Head Boys and Clive was Strutt House Captain.

In 1960 Mildmay did get given a few more than useful sportsman so apart from Ian and me there was Paul Biddlecombe, Steve Cawley, Dave Wood and others. Quite remarkably we are all stalwarts of the 1960 old boys' reunions and meet regularly, although our sporting prowess has dimmed somewhat! I am delighted to say that by the time we graduated to the sixth form Mildmay was "Cock House" for my last two year's at the school!

Talking to many of those old boys from that era it is sad that some have less fond memories of the schooldays than others. It was extremely competitive educationally, culturally and on the sports fields. It was quite a shock to be plunged into that environment even though I had been at a large school in Kings Road and it must have been much harder for those who came from the smaller village schools.

Overall though we could not ask anymore than what the school was able to provide for us and it remains a school of excellence even to this day. Many of us went on to be active members of the OCA and continue to enjoy what that fine organisation offers even to this day.

50 years on we feel privileged and 1960 ………? It seems just like yesterday!

4

WHAT'S IN A NAME?

Our 1960 intake of about 100 had about 40 different Christian names. The most popular were as follows: -

John 8%
Peter 7%
David 6%
Christopher 6%
Michael 5%
Martin 4%
Stephen 4%

So, this was fairly average for that baby boom era when naming the child was a little more adventurous, perhaps to do with the effect of television, but a long way removed from Wayne, Del, Darren and such but not yet into the modern era of the Josh, Sam, Cameron, Freddie, Harry and William etc.

Steve Little

One of the unusual Christian names in our year was Vaughan. Extremely uncommon at the time and still is today – perhaps he was named after Vaughn Williams the composer. However, for most of our school life we knew Vaughan Richmond as "Mitch" and many of us thought this was his real name! We did have a Harold with the unusual surname of Sprange but he was never a Harry but more often than not just Sprange! He was brainy so moved in different circles from me but was a quiet and likeable chap nonetheless.

So was Sweetman – the sort of boy who would not hurt a fly – but he had the unusual christian names of Rufus St. John. He unwittingly created an almighty stink when in the very early days in the first year someone scrawled in six-inch high letters R-U-F-U-S across his desk. It was so early in our time at the school that not everyone even knew his first name so the culprit would be from a small number of suspects.

Suddenly one day we were all kept in our classrooms at the Friars annexe and quizzed by the senior master there, Mr "Bill" Bloomfield, not someone to be messed with!

He first asked who knew what Sweetman's first name was so I put up my hand up along with about half a dozen others. We were not aware of what lie behind the question at that moment. I was a bit of a nosy so-and-so and I had seen his nametag inside his cap but that was all. It was enough though to be subject to the Bloomfield inquisition, which was a bit scary for an 11 year old! He was not wholly convinced of my innocence but I was and they never did find out whom it was who had scrawled on the desk (could it have been Sweetman himself perhaps?) but it was enough for us all to be stopped that day from enjoying mid-morning playtime and playing in the playground at lunchtime.

Talking of scrawling on desks, as we got much older there were two little phrases that appeared on countless desks around different classrooms at the main school.

First it was "IBV?" There was sudden rash of these appearing when we were in the fifth and sixth years and for a long time no one knew what they meant. It turned out that it stood for - Is Buzz Virile? Now "Buzz" was the nickname of Andrew Barton and it was a gentle taunt of his mates (possibly Cade or Dennis) but no one really knew who started it. No doubt it was a big joke to them but hardly anyone knew what its real meaning was and how it came about.

Second we had "Gia was ia!" This was a bit subtle as it was a clear play on words and referred to Eric Giachardi – another quiet, unassuming boy - but for years his name lived on at the school, at least for as long as those desks remained!

Some of the masters had nicknames and these are a few of the more unusual ones: -

"Noggs" Newman, "Rowdy" Yates, "Sparky" Hale, "Bruiser" Findlay, "Killer" Booth, "Rev" Franklin, "Mumbles" Turner, "Jake" Jackson, "Pinhead" Underhay, "Isaiah" (or "Tusker") Lee, "Larry" Kettle, "Tab" Hunter, "Hank" Marven, "Waxy" Wheatley and of course "The Pod" (the Headmaster, Mr Fanshawe).

Mr Lee ("Isaiah") was an interesting character, never seen not wearing his black gown; he swept round the school always looking out for and dealing with ill discipline. He never smiled but he was an excellent English teacher and about third in the hierarchy of the school behind the Head and his Deputy Mr Findlay. So "Bruiser" Findlay and "Isaiah" Lee were very much the men to deal with discipline or lack of it.

Mr Lee got one of his two nicknames because he had an eye defect, perhaps a war wound we did not know, but one eye looked in one direction and the other in a slightly different direction. When we were in our early years we would usually queue outside the classroom where we had our next lesson. This particular day we were noisy and pushing and shoving. Suddenly "Isaiah" came round the corner and shouted for quiet but the pushing continued. He walked straight towards me focusing right on me. He lifted his hand to cuff me round the ear, or so I thought, and I turned my head expecting a slap around my ear but he hit the boy two up the line from me. Clearly I had been looking into the eye not used for focussing!

As far as the boys were concerned there were very few interesting nicknames but Pete Ankers went through the school dreading a nickname but it never came and even with a name like Little, I was open to abuse but none came along, to my face at least!

There was "Stodge" Stoneham, "Otter" Ottley, "Gus" Gunn, "Froggy" Frost, "Cacky" Reeves, "Creepy" Cawley, "Dasher" Asher (his initial was D), "Buzz" Barton, "Brun" Brown, "Chisel" Stone, "Mitch" Richmond, "Dopey" Opie, "Seaweed" Seward and a few others.

However, we had an Alan Sole and in the early years we would always greet him with Ah…. Sole!

Then we had a Thompson and a Thomson. Of course, said the same but spelt differently. The latter was called "P-less", which later derived into the obvious!

"Dopey" Opie was to live up to his name once we got to the fourth year. He was a fairly bright lad but quiet in sort of creepy way. He was to fall foul of our English teacher and then of the school itself. "Dopey" had the habit of using apostrophes in his English essays that would always incur the wrath of the English Department. He would put "isn't" or "haven't" into his text. Not much of a writing crime today but in the mid-sixties it was almost a hanging offence! He then had the audacity to write, "ain't" in one of his literary efforts. Not only does this word use an apostrophe it was not an accepted word in any part of our language, even slang – at least according to the English master. This master on marking "Dopey's" essay the previous evening was apoplectic with rage the next day and as soon as he arrived in class he threw chalk at "Dopey" and then the board rubber. He tore poor "Dopey" off the most frightful strip for "ain't".

"Dopey" was never the same boy again and had an innate hatred of English. The following term we sat our mock O-levels in English Literature, which included the inevitable exposure to the plays of the Bard. No one liked studying them that much, least of all "Dopey". He exacted his revenge on the English Department when penning an answer in the exam about our appreciation of Shakespeare. Suffice to say that immediately after the marking of the papers "Dopey" was suspended from school for the offensive words used and the very nature of his comments on the detrimental effect the great man had on teenagers!

...

Unusual names were not just confined to KEGS. The simple minds of we teenagers could make anything seem hilarious (to us at least) and we would go on about any experience for days and weeks after. The fact that nearly fifty years later some of us recall that we once played cricket against a team that had twin boys called Glasscock playing against us, simply goes to show how the childish quirkiness of a name is still fondly remembered to this day!

Days We'll Remember All Our Lives

We were in the Under 15s cricket team and playing against Buckhurst Hill Grammar. We were interested to see their team listed in the scorebook had Glasscock P and Glasscock G batting at number six and seven.

Once they were five wickets down we had the two brothers batting together. In later experiences in life I came across someone called Glasscock, in fact he nearly bought my first house from me, but it was pronounced Glazz Co and not Glass Cock. So brothers P and G Glass Cock had to endure the most frightful sledging, which, whilst prevalent in cricket today, was virtually unheard of then.

"Stodge" fielding at first slip had us in teenage hysterics as he gave a mock John Arlott commentary on proceedings.

"Now we have two glass cocks striding out to the wicket and we can see them coming. We really do hope they have their protective boxes in place. Standing in their crease taking guard, one cock is slightly larger than the other but with a degree of massage the smaller one becomes the same size, or so the Buckhurst Hill captain tells us. Let's hope they are not "shattered" by the time they complete their innings. If they remain at the wicket for long they will become a "pane" to the KEGS team. And now Gunn comes into bowl and it's full of length and, oh dear, it has hit Glasscock P in the groin area and he's doubled up in agony but at least he's now got a ball to go with his cock. Biddlecombe is helping P and is wiping the nether region with a chamois and now all seems well.

Coming on at the pavilion end is Cawley who can bowl either an off break or a leg break but let's hope for Glasscock G that he does not bowl the middle break. Oh my god it is the middle break and it has gone straight on and hit G in the groin area just like his brother. Wait a minute he's standing there unmoved. The umpire has asked if he is all right. "Yes thank you," he says, "I've got double glazing!"

And so it went on. In fact they were not very good cricketers and did not stay at the crease for long but I often wonder if this verbal bullying did affect them in later life but perhaps they just became the Glazz Co brothers instead!

...

Radio provided us with as many catchphrases as the modern day. The "Goons" gave us names and phrases like "Ah this is Lady Poole and her son Cess" – "Round the Horn" at Sunday lunchtimes gave us double entendres by the bucket load and we would often go round on a Monday morning repeating, inanely, these catchphrases heard the day before. There was one such day when two pupils pretended to be telephoning each other. One was the manager of a football club telephoning the Football Association and the other would answer "Sweet, FA, here" – they thought it hilarious and it was for the rest of us up until about the third time we heard it but they carried on with it all day!

TV was appearing in more and more homes as the 60s got underway. Even then, Bruce Forsyth had a catchphrase as he introduced Sunday Night at the London Palladium. It was "I'm in Charge" which he used when he hosted the Beat the Clock game show for members of the audience, which formed a short part of the programme. We all adopted that phrase and even the teachers picked up on it and thought how "with it" they were by using it in class!

We were all aware of nicknames. The Tiger comic, one of the few that had some colour in it, had Roy of the Rovers as its main character. The front page was the only part that had colour and we eagerly awaited it to drop onto our mats through the letterbox each week to catch up with Roy and his best friend "Blackie" Gray – Blackie was actually white Caucasian!

Chalky White was common and many of these nicknames came from the days when young men did their National Service. The top TV comedy of the late 60s was "On The Buses" and its only coloured conductor was a "Chalky" White.

Many of our fathers' friends had nicknames. My Dad worked with a "Wanger" Clark – one can only guess at how he got this and I bumped into "Wanger's" son a few years back but he did not know exactly how his Dad came by that name!

There was "Swallow" Sheldrake, "Nobby" Clark, "Lofty" Doran, a lad known only as Yogi Bear who worked with my Dad and whom I trained with for football – I never knew his real name. My Dad was nicknamed "Tiggy" at school. I found out that this came about because in a children's story Teddy Bear's little son was "Tiggy Bear" and, as my Grandad was known, ironically I would say, as "Teddy Bear" Little that's how my Dad got that name.

On the radio we got to listen to the comic genius Stanley Unwin whose stock in trade was to pronounce words and names incorrectly but in such a way that you could still understand what he actually meant. This was extremely clever but sounded like he was sometimes pronouncing names backwards. Some of us, for a while at least, adopted this amongst our little group. The more amusing names in a sort of reverse order were those two "Polish boys", Ecneret Nitram Yeltek and his brother Trebor (Terence Martin and Robert Ketley) highly amusing, well it was to us at least! Another one we liked was Nnug Nai (not a member of the Viet Cong but Ian Gunn, of course!).

…

Even names within families had their idiosyncrasies and when I met my wife to be in 1967 I discovered that her father's name was George but everyone called him "John". His brothers were Harold and Alec and they were called "Bob" and "Pod". One sister was Gladys but always signed birthday and Christmas cards as "Georgy"! The other sister was Phyllis who went from farm worker's daughter to farm owner and did not succumb to a nickname in later life but when she was a schoolgirl she was known as "Sparrow" as she had sparrow-like legs!

One of my best friends at KEGS was Richard John Smith who was to become my Best Man when I married. His family trait was to give sons the same first name as their father. However, the family called the sons by their MIDDLE names so my friend was known as John at home. So whenever I phoned him and his Mum answered I had to remember to ask for John, not Richard, and that was difficult, as we all knew him then, and still do now, as Dick!

Dick was always the nickname for a Richard but perhaps for obvious reasons, it has dropped out of fashion. Even my old school friend Dick Green is back as a Richard nowadays.

We all know a Richard but no Dicks these days - younger Richards sometimes opt for Rick – I know of a Richard called Rick but his family call him Junior as his father is also a Richard! This Rick has the surname of Toogood and went out with a girl called Dix and they always said that if they got married they would be called Toogood-Dix – he married someone else!

...

Steve Little

These entendres were further illustrated when in the 60s I knew of someone whose surname was Ramsbottom and not liking its possible connotations changed it by deed poll to Pratt!

...

So the 100 or so boys with the variety of names settled into their KEGS school career to work hard and at the end of it all leave with the right qualifications to make a real NAME for themselves in the adult world!

5

THIS LATIN …… IT'S ALL GREEK TO ME!

One of the boys in our year was not the first in the history of education to utter in all innocence the immortal words, "This Latin … it's all Greek to me!"

Even our Latin master said how funny the comment was when it happened in our Latin class in 1960 although no doubt this was far from being the first time he had heard it.

At Primary School we had all learnt some French words and some of us had received lessons in the language.

To suddenly be thrust into Latin was more than just a little shock. We were told that we needed O-level Latin or we would not get a place at Oxford or was it Cambridge, or perhaps both. The fact that only ten per cent at best of the one hundred first year intake would ever get to Oxbridge why did the school not just choose the twenty or so likely candidates for Oxbridge and teach them Latin in the year up to O-level, our fifth year, to save us all from the purgatory of Latin declension?!

If they had told us that Bobby Charlton had got O-level Latin and had now become one of the most famous footballers in the world we would have queued up for extra lessons in the hope we could don the red of Manchester United and the white of England. Today we hear that England star Frank Lampard, ex of Brentwood Public School, has got GCSE Latin Grade A, so why are today's teenagers not falling over themselves to sign up for the Classics in the hope that it'll get them onto £120,000 a week at Chelsea and have any woman they could want when they get older?

In 1960 from our first week at KEGS we were into Latin. We were told of the school motto "Quicquid agas sapiens age fortiter ex animoque" ('Whatsoever thy hand findeth to do, do it with thy might') – the shortened version was "Fortiter ex animo" and we carried this around with us all the time as it was on the school badge on the front of our blazers. Twice each week we had Latin lessons. The first noun you learnt then was Mensa – a table – and the first verb was Amo – I love – so the first phrase we learnt was to love a table. No doubt a psychologist would have a field day with that now!

It did not get any better when we learnt the phrase for "Yes" was "Ita Vero" – much of Latin has gone into our language fortunately someone along the way thought Yes, Ya, Yep, OK, Oui and Si were seen as better alternatives.

From 1960 we had a motley selection of Latin masters. To start with it was either the "Rev" Franklin or "Waxy" Wheatley. To eleven year olds these two very fine old gentlemen looked as though they might have known Virgil personally. None of us was sure whether the "Rev" took church services on Sundays but before we could investigate further he retired, shortly to be followed by "Waxy".

David Dunkley was one of those who came in to replace the retirees and it was he that got me through Latin O-level. Sad to say I neither got to Oxbridge nor got offered a contract at Man United, Chelsea or any other club!

Further down the line came Ken "Killer" Booth to teach us not only Latin but Greek as well. "Killer" was as "Yorkshire" as they come and looked like he might have stoked furnaces in the steel works of Sheffield whilst studying Homer and Virgil. He was as strong as an ox and a pretty decent footballer. Many of us ended up playing alongside him in the Old Chelmsfordians' Olympian League side and he was your arch-typical centre forward in the Nat Lofthouse style and took no prisoners and particularly disliked goalkeepers who were not so protected then as they are now!

Steve Little

Ken was a great football coach to the all-conquering school team of the autumn of 1967 (we only played football up to Christmas when the school then reverted to the more effete game of hockey to satisfy those not good enough to make the school football teams!).

Ken would get us fit and so hard was his training that the slightly less fit players were often physically sick in trying to cope with his demanding routines. With another master, Dick Church, providing us with the technical coaching, we were indeed a formidable team winning all our matches against other schools, drawing with Corinthian Casuals and losing (unluckily) to the full first eleven of the Old Chelmsfordians. What is this to do with Latin, you might ask? Well we did play three matches away against Cambridge colleges – Gonville and Caius, Emmanuel and St Catherine's – and won them all by a street and found the study for our Latin O-levels useful, as Latin mottos and phrases seemed to adorn every wall in the colleges! So this was why to get into Oxford or Cambridge you need this damned O-level.

In fact, Latin does form the base for so many languages and is always helpful for doing crosswords or understanding a lot of the medical world! However, the best phrase the masters could have taught us right from day one and to help us accept what the world was to throw at us as we got older, was not "Amo mensa" to help with our verbs and nouns but "Illegitimus non carborundum est" – loosely translated as "Don't let the b*****ds grind you down".

6

BOXING – IT'LL MAKE A MAN OF YOU SON!

The school gym was small with wall bars around three sides. It had one entry half way down the long side, the windows were on the opposite side and overlooked the playground and beyond that the sports field. In the left hand corner of the gym was the storeroom and there arranged on hooks on the wall were the boxing gloves.

Their condition suggested they had been in use since before the Second World War and might even have been purchased from the Forces. National Service was still compulsory in 1960 but close to its end. Boxing was a major pastime in the Army and many of the good fighters that were around in the 1940s and 1950s learnt their trade there.

Steve Little

We young eleven year olds were used to football and cricket and then the next most energetic thing we did was maypole dancing!

Now, in PE lessons we were forced to don these "one size only" huge boxing gloves onto our small hands. Some gloves were bigger than our heads and we looked somewhat unbalanced with them on our hands.

Mr Pike was one of the PE masters and he looked like he could handle himself in the ring. He taught us our stance and how to throw a punch. We had sparring jousts. Boxing was commonly featured on TV and radio and we had a rich diet of fights to watch or listen to, be they professional or amateur. As my parents had a TV set, I thought I knew all the moves having watched Henry Cooper and Brian London exchange slinging left hooks on a regular basis. Then there was this American chap called Clay who had won Gold in the 1960 Olympics, he was supposed to be good.

My parents had bought me a sort of punch bag the previous Christmas. It had a red ball like thing on the top of a stand. It had a metal pole fixed into a wooden base, which you stood on so when you hit the ball the whole thing did not shoot across the room! We had had great fun with it that Christmas. My cousin, Brian, a big lad even then, was very adept at it for a boy of nine. His younger brother Keith was seven and much smaller in stature. He wanted a go so I placed my foot on the base to hold it in place and Keith took the most almighty swing at the ball and hit it flush. It was all I could do to stop the contraption falling over. Keith immediately turned to Brian and me and smiled in satisfaction. What he forgot was that, of course, the ball recoiled and it hit him straight on the temple and knocked him out. Brian and I brought Keith round. He was stunned but did not even cry. We told him not to tell anyone and so our parents never knew!

Anyway back to the action in the gym. The older boys from our Houses came and watched us one day and we were called to "trials" after school. "Tab" Hunter, one of the other PE masters, supervised these. He was a likeable chap and I got on well with him during that first term. I was aghast at Christmas when our first school reports came out. We were graded for each subject - A was Excellent, B was Good, C was Satisfactory, D was Weak and E was Very Poor. He gave me an E for PE! My father was apoplectic as he saw me as Tottenham Hotspur's new influential inside right or the new Raman Subba Row or perhaps Chris Chattaway when I got older. I did get my School Colours for football and cricket when I was older so Mr Hunter was proved wrong or perhaps it was an early wake up call for me!

Anyway he had seen me box so perhaps that is where he got the "Very Poor" from and he was right! However, this did not stop me from being selected for the Mildmay house boxing team representing the first year. I am not sure there was a weight class for me as I was only four feet eleven tall and weighed about six stone. I was drawn against Peter Gray who was in my class and he was representing Strutt house. The winner of our bout would fight the winner of Holland against Tindal.

Gray and me had some previous. We had a fight in the playground one day – the only time I can ever recall this happening to me. "Sod's law" meant we were to fight each other in the ring.

We had seconds in our corner who were older boys from our House and normally either Mr Pike or Mr Hunter would referee.

The fight was three, two-minute rounds and there were judges as I recall.

The fight was all a blur. I can still taste the disinfectant washed onto my face between rounds and was frightened when I saw the blood wiped from my cut lip at the end of the second round. I was told by my seconds that I might have lost the first two rounds so my only hope was to have a storming final round. The sight of the blood was my spur. Gray didn't know why I was now like a whirling dervish and when I got back to the corner I was heartily congratulated by the seconds but I still lost by two rounds to one, perhaps Mr Hunter was a judge!

I did secure one house point for Mildmay just for turning out and this went to our School year total. This was my first ever point of which there would be more over the years to come.

Days We'll Remember All Our Lives

Tindal always won the boxing house points match because although the selection was random as to which house you went into, if you were a boarder you were always in Tindal for some reason. Boarders living away from their homes were made of sterner stuff in my experience and perhaps this explained their prowess at boxing.

My house did have some stars even at age eleven. Ian Gunn was a strong lissom young lad who I had been with at Primary School. He was nicknamed "Gorgeous Gus" after the comic book character that had the hardest shot in football and still has that nickname almost fifty years later. He broke his wrist boxing against Peter Holmes (Tindal) but still won his bout. The diagnosis came after the fight.

Steve Robbins was another Mildmay lad and he had also been with me at Primary School. He lived on one of the toughest estates in Chelmsford but was fairly meek and mild. He achieved cult boxing status at the new school not because of his success in the ring but for the fact that he brought an end to boxing forever at the school.

During a bout he suddenly started shouting out that he could not see anything after one piece of action. "I've gone blind," he shouted, "I can't see." The masters and the senior houseboys present leapt into the ring and gently lowered him to the floor. His opponent was visibly shaken, "But I haven't hit him yet!" He was ignored. Robbins was carried away. An ambulance was called and he was treated at the hospital but gradually he said his sight was returning. In fact he later owned up to us that he had never lost it in the first place but this was the only way he could think of getting out of boxing.

Boxing never took place at the school again. Steve went on to have many a non-combative fight in his life to make the most of the chances the school's education gave him. He was from a relatively under privileged family and had a successful career but was, unfortunately, to pass away at a young age.

7

"AND LASTLY EITHER A HAMMER OR A BRUSH AND DON'T KICK THE SHAVINGS OUT OF THE DOOR WHEN YOU LEAVE"

These were the most blessed words heard in any week during our first two or three years at the school. Often no one heard Mr Danvers say anything beyond "brush" as we all slammed shut the cupboards containing the tools before he could finish his verbal check of the cupboard's contents but it at last signalled the end of a double period of woodwork.

The words never changed in all the years he was at the school.

What purgatory it all was! Out of 100 boys I can barely remember anyone who was a dab hand at planing bits of wood, making various joints that actually fitted together and nicely cutting through wood with a saw. The nearest we had ever got to using tools for such craftsmanship prior to going to the school was to move our Dad's ones out of the way to get our bikes or footballs out of the shed.

For our first ever lesson with us all resplendent in our aprons with our name in the top left hand corner with our Form and Set number beneath, Mr Danvers (or Major on Fridays when it was "Cadet Force" day) showed us how to plane a piece of rough wood that was about 13 inches long and two inches wide and an inch thick.

First of all we would saw the piece down to be 12 inches long, the task being to create a foot long ruler with the inches marked on it. Once one side was planed we would check with a setsquare that the whole length was as Mr Danvers called it "set straight and square" and take it to him. He would hold it up to the light, check it and if it were as he wanted it, he would put what he called a "face mark" on the side of wood. This "face mark" was like a straight line with a circle at the top and apparently was commonly used by carpenters.

You would return triumphantly to your bench receiving pats on the back and a few "well dones" to celebrate the completion of what was really a simple task only made difficult by those endeavouring to accomplish it!

This according to "Dan", as we called him, would be our first job of four that we needed to complete in the first academic year. Well, by Christmas most of us were still trying to get all four sides planed of our first task and have them "face marked" – this was still only half the job, the end product being the foot ruler. So, after having four sides "straight and square" we had to etch the lines denoting each inch and then using a sharp-ended tool insert the 1, 2, 3 and so on as the inch record. Once it was completed "Dan" made another inspection and if satisfied would allow us to take it home to our parents. There are still boys from that time who have their rulers triumphantly retained in their possession this being a far greater prize to them now than a certificate for a grade A for A-level Chemistry!

If you messed up a piece of wood "Dan" would replace it. Many of us planed away and got turned down for a "face mark" time and again. By that time our intended rulers would only be useful to our Mums as knitting needles so we had to get a replacement piece. "Dan" would mark in his register how many you used. I think it was after two you got a "Ticket Warning" and if you messed up number three in the same school year you would get a "Ticket".

Steve Little

To most of us a "Ticket" was an anathema. It was a sign of failure. It was a sheet of paper with a table of a school week split into the 40-minute lesson segments and one at the bottom of each column to be signed off by the parents each night to confirm you had completed your homework. Into the table we had to write in the lessons or the "Office" typed them in and the Master would sign that you had attended his lesson, insert a comment or test results etc. This you would carry round for the whole week then have it signed off by the Head or his Deputy. If you kept your nose clean you would never get a "Ticket" but in woodwork it was just that we were all naff at what we were doing and, seemingly beyond our control, we would suffer the ignominy of a "Ticket".

I remember spending about six double woodwork lessons pretending to plane my piece of wood to complete one of the tasks. It was the size of yet another knitting needle and I had had my "Ticket" warning and so there was no chance of another piece of wood and I was determined not to get the dreaded piece of paper. By the time my knitting needle had almost become the width of a toothpick I recall I went home to my Nan's for lunch before one woodwork lesson and feigned illness with a hacking cough but she did not buy the ruse and gave me a cough sweet to suck instead! The cough soon went when I walked back to the school to try and outwit "Dan". The good thing was he rarely got out of the chair behind his desk that was right at the end of the rectangular workshop and my bench was at the other end. It never occurred to me that all this grief could be overcome if I just went down to Browns the local timber yard and got them to knock up a piece of two by one with the sides and edges "straight and square" for the cost of a few measly pence out of my pocket money. It would be easy to copy "Dan's" "face marks" and smuggle it into the workshop. How naïve, yet honest, we were!

Safe to say I never did get a "Ticket" from "Dan" as the end of the school year came to my rescue.

With the ruler completed I moved onto another job, which was to test our ability to make a basic joint, and the thing looked like an ashtray except mine didn't and whilst "Dan" signed it off I was not allowed to take it home as it was not of sufficient standard.

It was the same with the third job that was a test to create a mortise and tenon joint. It again just passed muster but stayed at the school and probably went into "Dan's" waste bin in his storeroom and joined my "ashtray".

My pride and joy was a box with a lid and a little knob on the top. I managed to complete this at the beginning of the third year (I was supposed to have completed it by the end of the first of course!). By now I had moved on from "Dan" and was under the watchful eye of Mr Pike and this slightly improved my skills but I was rarely out of the bottom quartile in terms of ability in my Set. He gave me "Satisfactory" for each of the three school reports from my third academic year but might have something to do with the fact that I was in his "House" and he was also a Sports Master and I was decent at football and cricket by then.

Despite my wife's pleading to throw away my old school reports and such like, I knew they would come in handy one day! I have searched out "Dan's" comments and marks for the two academic years of the purgatory that was Woodwork:

Term	Term Position	Attainment	Industry	Comments
Autumn 1960	14/25	C (Satisfactory)	C	Fair Progress
Spring 1961	22/25	D (Weak)	D (and ringed in red by the Head)	He must work much harder
Summer 1961	24/25	D	D	Weak
Autumn 1961	24/24	D	D (ringed again!)	Very weak
Spring 1962	21	D	C-	Improvement is slight
Summer 1962	17/24	C	C	Some improvement

So I am proud to say that I did actually get better or it might be that others got worse!

Mr Danvers passed away some time ago but he might be looking down on me benignly if he has seen the stud wall I have put up splitting one of our rooms at home into two. Sorry to say I did not use any of the joints he taught us and found a screw does the job just as well BUT I never did kick the shavings out of the door!

8

ART FOR ART'S SAKE?

A good friend of mine went to Grammar School in Bradford in the 1950s. He liked Art lessons and was always disappointed not to come top of the class – it was not until a few years later that he noticed in the Press that the boy who came top every time ahead of him had done quite well for himself in the art world – he was David Hockney!

So talent is around us now and has been at various times in the past. This was not the case for the 1960 intake at KEGS, Chelmsford, however!

You are either good at art or you are not – it is rarely something you can teach a youngster to do unless they have some talent in the first place. It must be soul destroying for a master who must be a talented artist himself to have 25 boys in Set 3 for Art who have absolutely no talent for his subject whatsoever.

It is clear that sportsmen are rarely any good at art (Jack Russell the cricketer is an exception but he, by his own admission, is a little eccentric and not your archetypal sports star) and we had in Set 3 a decent amount of sportsmen. We also had the occasional boy bent on mischief and he would never want to learn anyway. Then there were those that would give it a go but this was probably only about 6 out of the class of 25 and really they never did get any better!

Art – or Double Art as we called it because it was always for two lesson periods of forty minutes each – was not purgatory like Woodwork but something we just put up with and probably did try to master just a little bit.

Whilst we talk of masters for Art some of us actually had a lady teacher for our first year. She was Connie Alderton. She was a legend in her time at the school but she was due to retire at the end of our first year and duly did so.

Other masters came and were probably equally disillusioned by our lack of talent as Connie Alderton would have been. By the time we got to the Third Year only a few of us actually looked forward to Art lessons but it was a little piece of respite from the rigours of Latin, Maths, Physics and Chemistry and certainly better fun than planing a piece of wood down to a sliver whilst trying to make something that would at best be fairly useless anyway!

Poor Mr Noble arrived to take us for Double Art in the Third Year. We are now rising 14 year olds, talentless at Art and more bent on mischief than looking to follow in the footsteps of Mr Hockney.

Now Mr Noble was a gentleman who was certainly nearing the end of his career. To most of us he was like a kindly grandfather and certainly looked as old as mine. We unmercifully took advantage of him. Why is it that school children will pick up on a teacher's weakness and play to that? It is embarrassing to think of it now as far as Mr Noble is concerned because he had a hearing problem and wore a hearing aid in one ear.

It was not one of these subtle aids you see today just behind the ear or fixed to glasses. It was the old fashioned type with a lead down to the sound box that he had fixed to the belt around the top of his trousers. It was just like he was listening on his transistor to one of the pirate radio stations of the time! He was often asked by some of the boys what was this week's number one but he could not fathom out what we meant!

Whilst we were sitting at our desks he would walk round looking at our attempts at whatever this week's subject was. The seasonal changes to the trees outside the art room were often a subject dear to Mr Noble's heart and we all had a go at bringing joy to his heart but normally failed dismally. Some of the more "mature" boys asked him if we could have a "live" subject to sketch one week during the year.

Steve Little

He declined but failed to realise that the boys had in mind a couple of girls from the High School that they might like to sketch in the style of some of the great Italian Masters i.e. without any clothing on!

When he stood next to you tutting at our attempts at the autumn leaves on the oak tree outside we would often turn to ask a question of him. It would be perfectly timed for when his sound box was directly adjacent to your mouth. Your lips were close to the leather-bound box and the voice was raised to quite a few decibels higher than you would normally use in a classroom. This caused Mr Noble to jump a mile and immediately turn down his volume control believing that someone must have turned it up or there was a mal-function.

Of course, sometimes somebody had indeed fiddled with his volume control. Whilst he was distracted with one boy another would creep up and turn up the volume control so the combination of this and the raised voice would be most uncomfortable for him.

This was not all. Being a double period lesson the school bell would go halfway through. For the whole of that school year the class would stand up when the bell went. We would stop work as if on strike. At first Mr Noble seemed unaware of what was happening but as we did it each week and for week after week after week he just accepted it. After we had remained standing for a good five minutes he would tell us it was now time to sit down. No tantrum or disciplining - it just became a part of the norm.

How cruel it all was but most of us thought it a hoot. Sorry Mr Noble. You were a kind and gentle man.

9

YOU'RE IN THE ARMY NOW, LAD – WELL, AT LEAST FOR ONE DAY A WEEK!

By September 1962 we were entering our third year. Frank Ifield had topped the charts for some weeks with the yodelling "I Remember You". A third of the boys, the brighter ones, from our first year did two year's schoolwork in one during our second year and jumped to the fourth year. Complicated yes but it was fast streaming to O and A levels for some reason. However, we were all eligible now to join the Combined Cadet Force (CCF).

So from that September, only those delicate ones chose not to join the CCF. National Service had not long ended in 1960 and whilst we were all born after the War it had only ended 17 years before in 1945. Most of our fathers and even grandfathers

Days We'll Remember All Our Lives

had been involved in it plus Chelmsford with its large manufacturing base had been a target for German bombers and suffered quite badly, so most of our families had first hand experience of the war.

In 1962, the newspapers, radio and television were full of stories about the Cuban Missile crisis and the stand off between the US and USSR. Matters came to a head in that September and October.

A little like the rush to sign up in 1914 we third years flocked to sign up for the CCF, with the undoubted approval of our parents brought up on war. There were less than 10% of our year that joined what could be called the conscientious objector's section but the rest thought that messing about in khaki was preferable to having extra lessons, which is what the "objectors" had to face!

Each Friday throughout the school year we had to wear our full CCF uniform. This meant sitting through lessons in rather uncomfortable clothes before going on parade in the afternoon. The "objectors" went for their extra lessons but we "soldiers" refrained from giving them a white feather each!!

The CCF had its own hut in the school grounds that served as a bolthole for the officers and also housed the quartermaster's stores. All sixty or so new recruits had to be kitted out and the boys from other years got their replacement kit at the beginning of this new school year as they had all grown out of their uniform over the previous year. We collected the "hand-medowns" and hoped they had been cleaned during the summer!

We had a black beret, two khaki shirts, army tie, standard army issue tunic and trousers, gaiters and army belt. Our parents were expected to buy us new army boots. So the next weekend we spent the Saturday in Millets getting fitted up.

At our first parade when we picked up our equipment, we were shown how to look after our kit. We were shown how to blanco our gaiters and belt. Most of the boots had dimpled uppers and in order to get a good shine we were encouraged (nay, told) to heat up a tablespoon and then place it on the toe cap so that the small dimples disappeared and we were left with a smooth toe so we could polish it in such a way that "you can see your bloody faces in it" as the NCOs told us.

Some of us could never master the most effective blancoing technique whereas some boys looked like professionals in their appearance. Milton was one such and not surprisingly he went on to join the Marines from the school and ended up a Major General and their commanding officer!

The gaiters were wrapped round your ankles and your trousers tucked into them in traditional army style. Some boys used elastic bands inside the trousers to get a neat tuck and some used ball bearings to weigh the trousers down to get an even neater finish. Fortunately the Hoffman ball bearing factory was just down the road from the school so there was no shortage of supply as we all knew someone who worked there who could get balls for us that had fallen off the production line!

The CCF only had a few officers and they were our schoolmasters. The senior officer was Major Danvers who in "Civvy Street" was E B Danvers, "Dan" the dreaded woodwork man. We did not see much of him when we were on parade each Friday and most of us were not sure what he did for the CCF but there was the occasional big full dress parade, a camp during the summer holidays and the Corps of Drums to organise and supervise. The boys in the Corps of Drums band were the really keen ones. They would practise one night of the week and then give a full commitment on a Saturday, particularly in the summer months, when they would play at carnivals, fetes and so on. We were, in fact, very proud of them because they really were very good and had the accolade of more than once leading the Chelmsford carnival, one of the biggest events in Essex at that time. In view of the weekend commitment you rarely found the band included sportsmen because they preferred the cricket and athletics fields or the tennis courts on summer Saturdays.

Corps of Drums

Many of us fancied playing the drums but the call of sport held sway.

Thursday evening saw an added hour of homework for all the "soldiers", as we had to get out the duraglit and polish our cap badges, belt buckles and those small buckles on the gaiters. Then we had to blanco our belts and gaiters and polish our boots. Our Mums would iron the trousers so we could almost cut our fingers as we ran them along the seams.

On the Friday morning many would walk to school often joining up with others. Some of us had to pass the Girl's High School a quarter of a mile up the road from KEGS. Now girls are supposed to fancy men in uniform but we got more laughs in our direction than alluring glances. So that was our first obstacle. The next one was the fact that we were inspected at the main school gates by a couple of NCOs, normally sixth formers. They would make sure we smartened ourselves up and if improperly dressed we would be "on a charge" and had to do fatigues in the afternoon when the rest did their drills.

All this was a little daunting to a 14 year old but there was often some "old lags" from the upper years that could help you out with some dodges. One was to enter the school by another means as opposed to the front main gate thus avoiding the inspection. Fortunately the NCOs did not in our time record your inspection and tick a register so it was fairly easy to avoid them.

The uniforms we wore were typically uncomfortable and even more so during the hot summer days but even in the winter the classrooms were so hot that things did not feel any better.

And so to the Friday afternoons. We "fell in" having been sorted into platoons in our first week. We had a Corporal and Sergeant in charge of us. Some were decent chaps but others took on the mantle of the type of NCOs seen in war films prevalent at that time. Haldane, we recall, was one such and would have been an atypical RSM with a bristling moustache, if only he could have grown one! He had the peaked hat that shaded his eyes and almost looked the part. Definitely more the Sergeant Major from "It Ain't Half Hot Mum" than Sergeant Wilson from "Dad's Army".

Many of us had the attributes of young Private Pike but some even had the drill skills of Corporal Jones in that they were always one beat behind the rest of us. Some even turned to their left when ordered to do a right turn and were thought by the rest of us to be somewhat effeminate as a result!

The whole experience was a little like National Service in that all we seemed to do was drill. We all had a mini passing out parade when we had to be individually dismissed from the squad, march up to an Officer, come to attention, salute, about turn and return to the squad. Those messing it up would get extra drill and have to do it again. For so called intelligent people we had a lot of poor soldiers. Many marched with their right arm in time with their right foot instead of the left and that made them look like a robot! Others just could not master the most basic of commands.

Mr Khrushchev and his Russian soldiers would have been quaking in their boots in Moscow if they knew that this was the flower of British youth and the next generation of soldiers they could be facing if the Cold War escalated into armed combat!!

By the time the summer of 1963 came along the Cuban crisis had abated but quite a lot of our winter "training" in the CCF had been curtailed by the freezing weather, for over three months from

Christmas until March the country was in the grip of the Big Freeze and global "colding" was believed to be on the way!

Traditionally, each summer the CCF had its big day. The whole force would parade on Westfields next to the school buildings and some eminent General from a local regiment would come down to inspect us much like the Queen did to her men at the Trooping of the Colour. Parents would come to watch, mostly mums, as dads would never be able to get time off work. The Corps of Drums would lead the display and we had spent weeks practising our marching making sure we kept in time to the big drum. On the day, we marched past the General and Major Danvers and the other Officers having learnt to do an "Eyes left" in rehearsal - as usual, the Corporal Jones clones got it wrong.

One of the pastimes of a young teenager with nothing better to do was to sit and watch the Trooping of the Colour and count the number of soldiers who collapsed in the heat of June and had to be carried off Horse Guards' parade. Now, however, it was our turn in full uniform on what was always the hottest day of the year to go through what the young men in their bearskins had to face.

One of our better "soldiers" was John Mayhew and he belonged to another pseudo military group outside of school and gave us all tips on how not to faint. Some either did not heed his advice or just could not cope and ended up on the grass. Ironically, even

Mayhew in attempting a right turn faltered but just about recovered his composure and carried on but he took a bit of stick about it later.

The end of the school year came and most of us felt better for the experience and so signed up for the summer 10-day camp in Scotland. It was to prove a little like those happy souls who went off to the trenches in 1914 only to find out that it was not quite what they thought it would be like. So proved the camp but then that's another story!

10

THE WORST WEEK OF MY LIFE...? WELL, AT LEAST WE MISSED RONNIE BIGGS AND HIS MATES!

"Look, why don't we all go to Cadet Camp in the summer it'll be a right laugh," said Dick Green.

"What - all that bloody marching and living in a field without proper bogs, no thank you," said "Stodge" Stoneham, "you won't get me there."

"Me, neither," said I, "I'm going to Somerset with my Mum and Dad, that'll do me!"

Mid-August 1963, Chelmsford Railway station, Monday afternoon five o'clock and a sizeable group of boy soldiers come together carrying kitbags bigger than them. There is "Stodge" who greets me with a shrug and a nod. Dick Green is his usual immaculate self. Then there's the resourceful Mills the boarder our only known smoker. We never actually saw him smoke in and around school but he always smelt of cigarettes. Then there was me. All were dressed in our army uniforms.

Mum and Dad had left for Somerset on the previous Saturday. "Fluff" Freeman confirmed the Searchers and their "Sweets for my Sweet" was this week's top of the pops. The departure of my parents left me, aged 14, alone for the first time ever, unless you count the nights spent at Nan's when Mum and Dad went to a dance. I had spent Sunday and most of Monday with my cousin Hazel, husband Brian and young daughter Julie.

Hazel was struggling with her blood pressure in the heat of August but she managed to make me enough sandwiches to last for the journey from Chelmsford to Fort William in Scotland via London, Crewe and Glasgow. These sandwiches were right at the top of my kitbag accompanied by a bottle of lemonade. Brian drove me to the station in his old black car with its odd doors that opened outwards from the front as opposed to opening from the back as with most cars.

Waving goodbye brought a lump to my throat – alone for the first time ever. Whilst "Stodge", Dick and the others were good mates they were not my Mum and Dad and at that moment I just wished I was in

Wedmore in Somerset with them enjoying a Vimto and a packet of crisps at The George.

Looking beyond the first group there was "Dil" Dowsett, a strong lad but not one of life's natural athletes, how would he cope with the rigours that lay ahead? Next to him was Chris "Seaweed" Seward, who was a lot smaller than me and looked ridiculous in a uniform about three sizes too big for him.

We all greeted each other in that non-committal way with the gruff "All right?" without expecting an answer. A few minutes passed and then suddenly we were called together by one of our NCOs. We stood to attention with our kitbags by our sides. We were told to pick them up and march in formation up the stairs to the "Up" platform and wait for the 5.15 to Liverpool Street.

The only memorable aspect of this part of the journey and that up to Kings Cross was that I ate about half of Hazel's sandwiches. This made me feel better but was to prove a big mistake as the journey wore on.

At Kings Cross we got aboard the Glasgow train but not before we had dropped off our kitbags at the luggage carriage. We were told to take out our sandwiches and everything else we might need for the journey, which would be overnight.

We were shown to our carriage and it was a corridor train and we had a compartment between six of us with a sliding door. No overnight sleeper train with proper beds for us and a steward to provide for our every need. All I had was Hazel's sandwiches and the lemonade. How stupid not to bring a book. Some did bring magazines but they were all read before we got to Rugby!

"Seaweed" had a book. A bloody train spotter's manual with all the diesel numbers and steam train names and numbers. He kept running up and down the corridor, with another enthusiast, spotting and then crossing off the train numbers as we passed them parked up or as they went past us. "Ooh a D67er," he would shout and write down the five-digit number, then cross through this in his little book. The remaining five of us pushed up the four armrests in the compartment so it gave us a bit more room to spread out. Remember this was a hot August night and we had our thick army uniforms on and from very early on we knew we would be in for an uncomfortable night. Some of the boys had been to camp with the cubs and scouts and were used to this jolly togetherness in a confined space or maybe they had brothers and sisters at home and shared bedrooms or just space there generally. For me, the unspoilt only child, this was a new and not very pleasant experience.

At least "Stodge" was there with me so I had one mate nearby. "Seaweed" continued with his relentless pursuit of numbers and even had us looking out for some on the other side of the train for him.

Being only 14 we were still polite young men but a couple of years on and we would have told him where to stick his train spotter's book!

Just as my last sandwich went and we were still south of Birmingham one of the sixth formers, an NCO, came round to check on us. We asked him what time we would get to Glasgow. He said 6.30 in the morning. We looked at each other in shock. But, we all said, in only takes about 5 hours to get there and it's 9 o'clock in the evening - which way are we going, via Penzance? "You'll see" was the only response we got from him.

What about having a wash and cleaning my teeth? Something I had done every evening for nearly 14 years? My stuff is in the kitbag so that's no use. All I could do was wash my face in the minute sink in the toilet before I had a wee and decided that at 10.30 it was time for sleep.

At about 11 we stopped. "Seaweed" told us this is a siding at Crewe – one of the busiest stations in the world being such a major junction. He was almost wetting himself with excitement. D67ers proliferate in that neck of the woods and he was to stay on watch throughout the whole time we were stationary which turned out to be about four hours and we were not even in the station but tucked into the sidings! So this is what the NCO meant by wait and see!

With "Seaweed" in the corridor spotting, the remaining five tried to make ourselves comfortable.

"Stodge" got into the luggage rack which was a netting affair strung across three supports over the width of the compartment. Even though only 14 "Stodge" was a decent size and on his way into the netting accidentally kicked one of the compartment lights and smashed it, showering the boy sitting beneath with glass. Another boy slept across one line of seats and one on the other with another stretched out on the floor. The fifth squeezed in a sitting position on one of the seats.

If "Seaweed" came into the compartment once, he came in a hundred times to tell us of his latest spot. Just before we eventually moved on from Crewe, Mills in the next compartment threatened to throw "Seaweed" out of the window if he didn't shut up and we all volunteered to help. The trouble was once the boy stopped spotting he demanded room in the compartment. We told him to get up into the luggage netting opposite "Stodge" and shut up but mind the lampshade when he did so. Being the smallest of us by far he had no alternative but to agree.

None of us could sleep. The strangeness of all this and, earlier on, Seaweed's constant interruptions meant it was now 4 in the morning and the sky was getting lighter. No sleep, no food, no money to go to the buffet car, we had never been up at this time of the morning either from a late night or just an early start. It was about now that I wished I really had gone to Somerset with Mum and Dad. And we hadn't got to the damn camp yet – what on earth was that going to be like?

At about 7 we got to Glasgow. I felt sick. It was probably the tiredness or maybe the anxiety of about what lay ahead. We disembarked and looked a right rabble. The compartment looked like a soccer-special where the hooligans had run amok. Yet any damage had really been only accidental but it did look bad.

We were taken to a café and told to order some breakfast. However there was a price limit so being the school/army that did not amount to very much! I still felt sick and, though seemingly dying of hunger, could not face anything apart from a coffee. We now had a few hours to kill so we were allowed to investigate that part of Glasgow. In 1963 the city was awfully run down. All the buildings, even on this bright summer's day, looked grey and drab. So did the people, who scurried off to work. Occasionally we got some strange looks as this motley group of boys from 14 to 18 ambled about. God help us if there's another war one local was heard to say!

I did manage a chocolate bar but felt so tired. At last the train to take us to Fort William arrived. In fact it was two trains in that we needed two steam engines to get us up the hills and mountainsides. "Seaweed" was ecstatic!

This was not the same sort of carriage. This time we had four seats around a table and I was able to get my head down on the table and go to sleep. The problem was I went into such a deep sleep I felt worse than before when "Stodge" shook me awake when we got to our destination.

From Fort William we were to travel the few short miles to Glen Nevis where our advance party of an Officer (a master) and some sixth formers had travelled up by lorry a few days earlier to pitch the camp.

It was late afternoon when we got there and Major Danvers welcomed us. The NCOs showed us round. There would be eight of us to a tent. A cursory glance inside showed it smaller than the train compartment without the headroom and we had to fit in two more people!

We were right next to a typical Scottish stream running low across the stones and other glacial debris. That was pleasant but, of course, at that time of year the midges take perverse delight in feeding on everyone and washing down the blood sucked from the poor victim with a quick drink from the stream.

Army surplus insect repellent was dished out to us. I am sure it was left over from the Africa Campaign all those years before because there was Egyptian type writing on the side. Probably bought as a job lot after the War ended we all agreed!

All this seemed not too bad until we were shown the latrines. There were four rectangular sides of canvass about five feet high with a small gap to go through. Inside, there were six "boxes" lined up in a neat row. Each had a lid and on lifting this there appeared a sort of seat for the user. We dared not look into them but suffice to say that over 45 years later the locals still talk about how long the grass was in that area in the spring of 1964!

Dick Green asked where the washing block was. The NCO looked at him as if he was mad. He pointed over towards the stream, "Over there you dimwit!"

We then went to the mess tent with its open sides and rows of tables and benches. We had a welcome cup of tea and a lovely piece of Dundee cake. I didn't feel sick anymore.

The 30 or so of us were then briefed on what the week or so entailed. The older boys would go off on overnight treks to places like the Isle of Skye but we younger ones would firstly have the chance to walk up the easy route to the summit of Ben Nevis. The next day after that, Thursday, we would be shown how to read maps and use a compass whilst on a trek up the Glen where we would bivouac (this was a brand new word for me at the time and didn't sound overly comfortable). This would be overnight and we would return to camp on the Friday. Saturday we would be taken out to different points all over this part of Scotland having been split into groups. We would be given all sorts of different map references and compass readings and we would have to go to each point. Finally, we would then all meet up at the final point and from there be picked up by one of our lorries and be brought back to the camp. Sunday would be a rest day or "leave" as we were told to say. That would normally be fine but "leave" in Fort

William on a Sunday? Not a lot going for it, as we were to find out. All but one solitary café was shut.

All that was in the future and details of what was planned for the remaining days would be conveyed to us in due course.

Anyway it is our first night in camp and we had to unpack our kitbag. We had a metal dinner plate onto which our Dads had etched our names. Likewise we had our names scratched onto knife, fork and spoon plus our boot cleaning brushes. There was a wash bag with flannel, soap, toothpaste and toothbrush. A writing pad and pen so I could send Mum and Dad a letter whilst they were in Somerset. I felt like writing one there and then and saying come and get me out of here! We had to bring a toilet roll but for me it was one of those neat pull out one sheet jobs but then I thought I won't be needing this as I have no intention of using those toilets for the next ten days, thank you very much! A towel was also there and something to wear in bed.

One good thing (sic) about the Army is that you don't need to take much clothing as you have the one uniform and your denim type fatigues for climbing Nevis and such like and a change of pants and perhaps a vest if your Mum said you must take it to Scotland because the weather's often bad there. With the temperatures currently in the 80s it seemed a little unnecessary!

It's quite late by the time it gets dark in the Glen at that time of the year so having doused ourselves in repellent an NCO came and showed us how we would be expected to leave our beds when we get up the next morning. Blankets had to be tucked in a certain way around your sleeping bag. Spotless boots had to be placed on top of your towel with the billycan, into which our food would be dropped at meal times; placed neatly in front would be the plate and cutlery next to it.

Some of us then played cards in the tent using a candle when the light finally faded. Those of us who had diligent personal hygiene standards went and brushed their teeth on the banks of the stream.

Back in the tent Seward was already asleep probably dreaming of another D67er, Mills rolled his fags and smoked them like the good chain smoker he was. We knew why he rolled his own – they looked so thin and uninviting plus he had licked the fag paper when he rolled it around the tobacco and so it was highly unlikely anyone would want one. This saved him from having to offer then round like he would if it was a packet of twenty. Actually, few of us smoked anyway, apart perhaps to nick one of our Mum's Players No 6 for a dare.

We had a chat about the journey and what lay ahead in perhaps the same way as those poor souls had done before being sent up to the frontline to do battle the next day, just like our fathers and grandfathers might have done during the two World Wars.

Steve Little

I began to settle down in my sleeping bag when my tummy gurgled and I felt that sensation you get when your body is telling you it's time to deposit some surplus down a toilet. This was not in my plan of abstaining for the whole ten days.

I got up and opened the tent flap making the normal teenage joke of, "I'm just going outside but I may be gone some time," echoing James Robertson Justice's famous last words as Titus Oates in the recent film "Scott of the Antarctic".

Looking across to the latrines my heart sank. There was a boy already there and I could see his head sticking above the canvass surround. Although there were another five boxes available to sit on I was not sharing this particular ablution with anyone. I did think about using the Officer's latrine, which I had spotted earlier but if caught there it would mean being placed on a charge and almost certain "jankers".

After a minute or so the boy got up and left and I started across to the gap in the canvass. Suddenly from my right a figure was running towards the latrine. It was a fifth-former who looked like he was caught short. I told myself I'm not going there now and returned to the tent and decided to try and save myself until the dead of night when I might get there and perform without an audience. I worked out that I was two when I last had an audience when I was doing a Number Two!

At about three in the morning I could wait no longer. "Stodge" got up to have a wee just outside the tent and I nipped over to the latrine. Bliss – absolute bliss!

It was barely light in the morning when there was a loud banging on the side of the tent. "Wakey, Wakey rise and shine the sun's burning yer bleeding eyeballs out!"

It was two of the NCOs. But we had just gone to sleep it couldn't be that time already, surely?

"Come on, come on, move yourselves. Get washed and changed and get your kit ready for inspection then it'll be breakfast at 07.30 hours." We all moaned but got dressed then went down to the river. It was a warm morning. Perfect for climbing mountains. The water in the stream was beautifully clear and cold and we washed our faces and smoothed our hair. No mirrors around to get our mops just how we liked so we didn't even bother with a comb.

We went back to the tent and sorted out our kit as we had been shown the night before. Mills, ever resourceful, knew exactly what to do and even though he was a scruffy looking fellow had his kit set out perfectly. Seward never got the hang of how to do it the whole time we were there and, being the smallest of us, got picked on unmercifully by the NCOs.

And so to breakfast. We had picked up our billycans, plates and cutlery and stood in a line outside the mess tent. Roger Bird was there. He was about six feet twenty seven and towered above me but then he was a sixth-former. He had a few words with me as we lived close to one another on the Woodhall Estate and often walked the couple of miles to school each day along with Terry Ketley. We also often went together to watch Chelmsford City play, hardly ever missing a home game for either first team or reserves. Birdie did not want to be seen mixing with the young ones but gave me a pleasant, "All right?" that morning.

He was serving up the tomatoes to go with the rather unusual looking fried eggs, which had already been slapped onto our plates. The tomatoes were in a huge saucepan almost the size of a baby's bath. It looked like tomato soup. We now knew why we had a billycan as this could take this sloppy mess whereas it would just have run off our plates! Whilst it had the redness of tomato it tasted nothing like tomato. I had only ever had school dinners for my first few months at Primary School and was more used to my Nan's excellent cooking for my main meal of a school day so this was a shock to taste something I would have guessed school dinners might be like. However, "Stodge" said that even Mrs Springett in the school canteen would be embarrassed serving up this dross!

A piece of bread was handy in that we could use it to mop up the red stuff and the egg yoke if indeed it was runny enough to actually mop up, which in most cases it most certainly was not. Another huge bath like container had a whole pile of bacon in it but it looked mainly rind and fat. It was slopped onto our plates. Green thought it was another lot of army surplus and probably got left over from when Hitler caved in during 1945. A cup of something brown that passed as tea helped wash it down and as we were so hungry we woofed it all down and even had seconds.

We were dismissed and told to be back on parade in fifteen minutes. The night before we had been given a small haversack and a water bottle that we were to fill up with drinking water from the large army issue containers just outside the mess tent. This we did. Mills took a sip and spat it out. They've put the water in with the petrol he exclaimed. We all took a sip and agreed. "Stodge" poured some into the palm of his hand and showed everyone the oil floating in it. Before we could do anything about it we were ordered to report to the lorry and brought to attention and loaded up. We only went a short distance along the road towards Fort William and then we were dropped off. Before us was the "easy" route to the summit of Ben Nevis, it did not look that easy to us! The older boys set off first and we brought up the rear.

It was a gentle climb but the temperature was already in the high sixties. We got about fifty feet up and Seward was sick and he was crying. He had vertigo and was close to fainting. One of the NCOs told him to pull himself together but another took pity on the young lad and escorted him back down and we carried on.

We were in our army kit but not the dress uniform but the fatigues that were thankfully a sort of denim and much lighter and thinner. The temperatures soared and we were struggling. The path might be gentle but with army boots that chafed and a pack full of our sandwiches and a few odds and ends that weighed us down progress was very slow. After about two hours we stopped for a rest. Some of the less athletic were struggling. The older boys had long since disappeared ahead with their leaders. We were now about 2,000 feet up and this was about halfway. We were told to rest and an officer came over. He told us it had been decided that the heat was too much today and we would have to wait here for the older boys to come down from the summit. The looks on our faces were a picture as we saw this as a good result.

Some time in the early afternoon the older boys arrived back down to us and revealed that one of their number, David Rixon, had started running down the slope not far above us (despite all of us having been told quite severely that we were not to run downhill at any stage) and had got out of control, fallen and hurt his ribs. He was helped down and confined to camp thereafter in view of his injuries.

The older boys who made the summit regaled us with stories of having a snowball fight at the top. Bearing in mind that at halfway up we were still basking in

90 degrees of heat, we were not sure whether or not they were joking. They were rightly pleased with themselves but it was if they thought they were Hillary and Tensing and that no one had ever got to the summit of Ben Nevis before!

All the way up to this halfway point we had drank the water to cool us down but it was so awful that some of us squeezed the juice from the oranges we had been given for our lunch to try and give it some taste but all to no avail.

We got back to camp at about 5 and had the rest of the day to ourselves. Some stripped off and went for a swim upstream where there were some deep pools. Not being a strong swimmer I wimped out. To a boy we had all filled our water bottles from the stream after we had drank down cupped handfuls of the beautiful iced cool elixir! The swimmers came back after about an hour and horrified us all with the alarming news that there was a dead sheep about fifty yards upstream. It made us all feel a bit queasy but then we all agreed that water laced with rotting sheep was far superior to the awful stuff from the jerry cans that clearly had petrol in not that long before.

Another restless night followed. The insect repellent had run out already but the midges were still with us. An officer told us that they were expecting fresh supplies of the repellent. Quite where from we had no idea and as these supplies never did turn up we assumed the officer didn't know either.

The next day we marched off further up the Glen along the road to nowhere as it became a dead end when it met the steep mountain slope. The single highlight of this march was the sight of a Roche Moutonee ("Rock of Lamb"). Only if you have studied glaciation in Geography with "Noggs" Newman did you know what one of these was. It is a rock that looks like a joint of lamb i.e. jagged at one end and with a smooth slope at the other. We all agreed to immediately inform "Noggs" of our find when we went back to school in September.

From the road, we walked up a pass on rising ground. Fortunately there were no steep rocky slopes either side so Seward was safe from his vertigo but we made sure he never found out how far above sea level we were.

After about half hour of steady climbing on what was another very hot day we suddenly reached a plateau of open greenness and right at the end of this valley was a huge and wonderful waterfall. We carried on walking to the left of the waterfall and up onto some raised ground and it was there that we were shown how to build a bivouac. Not that difficult really it was just a groundsheet held up by two sticks and another groundsheet underneath to lie on. We at least had something to keep us covered up and warm. We cooked something by the fire and settled down for the night. I woke up at first light and right in front of me was about a dozen little midges but I took no notice. In the morning I was told my face looked like it was full of zits but these were insect bites and everyone else had the same. We were due to move off. We'd all had a disturbed night and were tired. Before we set off I needed a Number Two but of course we had no latrine here so off I went for some privacy. I found a bush, made my deposit but... Oh dear, do I use my handkerchief or just my hand or perhaps some of the wet grass. I chose the grass but used it gently!

On the walk back to main camp we were tired and irritable and the annoying NCOs failed to lift our spirits but it was Mills or perhaps Dowsett who said, "Come on lads let's march along proudly and confidently it'll all make us feel better."

He was right. We all stood to attention and formed proper lines of three. The NCOs took over and called the marching steps Left, Right and so on. Someone started up a song. "It's a long way to Tipperary." We did not know much beyond the first verse but the lifting of the spirits was quite something to behold. If this Cadet Camp taught me anything in life it is that with a concentrated effort as a group it was possible to overcome all sorts of pain and discomfort!

This being the high season in Scotland there were plenty of tourists that passed us on the way back to camp and they would be mighty proud to see the flower of British youth, even though some were only 14, looking so confident and mature. It stirred for some the memories of those First World War soldiers marching off to the trenches so full of hope and expectation. For them death was a likely outcome but to us this one little coming together as a unit almost certainly was a defining moment in our development as people.

We did not think too much about this at the time because when we got back to camp we were more concerned about the blisters on our feet from the march and the uncomfortable bites on our faces.

The next day we junior ranks were taken off in the lorry and dropped off at different points. There were five or six of us in our group. The task was to take the map and compass point references and plot a course back to a certain point where the lorry would pick us up in late afternoon. The trouble was the officer had given us a wrong second reference so that it did not make sense. It did not however take an Einstein to work out what was wrong and whilst Dick Green was no Einstein he knew what the error was and worked out what the route was and where the final pick up would be.

We did not agree with him mainly just to be difficult. If they can't get it right then we stay where we are, was our mantra. It's that Management Training course conundrum where your plane has crashed in the desert. As a group do you stay where you are or go to where you think you will be found? Green took two others and went off. The rest of us stayed behind.

We were wrong of course but quite frankly were tired and spent the day at rest. The lorry came and picked us up because Green had remembered the road route and told the driver where we were. When we got back to camp we were up before the officer in view of our lack of effort and were given a day of cookhouse fatigues on the Monday.

Sunday saw us have a day off in a largely closed Fort William. We did find a newspaper shop that was open for a while and brought the spicy News of the World. It was that time when the newspapers were full of the Profumo Affair and the trial of Stephen Ward. Page after page of sexual details of what went on in upper class society. We learnt all sorts of things. For example we had wondered for ages what a two-way mirror was. I thought it was one mirror set up to reflect into another so one could see round corners but now we all knew better.

Government intrigue, Russian agents, high-class prostitutes, Lords of the realm and all sorts.

This August Sunday was no different, pages and pages of details of the trial but, wait a minute, all the comments about Stephen Ward, a high-class physio, were now in the past tense. We had to ask the shop owner what had happened. Apparently, Ward had committed suicide in jail and the trial would be at an end. Bit of a shame as we 14 year olds thought this reporting was the best sex education we could get!

The rest of that Sunday was spent in the only place open in Fort William. It was a pleasant café run by a nice lady who was completely taken by us and allowed us to stay all day although we hardly spent a thing. We did have some coffee and the most wonderful shortbread, which is something I remember with fondness to this day.

Monday arrived and I was on cookhouse fatigues, peeling potatoes and shredding tomatoes into the normal slush. This lasted all day. The rest of the boys went off on some exercise. Now what a result my indiscretions had got for me! From about 10 in the morning the hot weather came to an end and the heavens opened. Several months of rain fell in that one day it seemed. The boys came back early and looked a bedraggled bunch looking like refugees from the trenches at Passchendaele.

Did I laugh? Of course I did.

I helped serve the Scotch Mutton (the only meat we ever saw) with the tomato slush and potatoes. In view of the low morale we were allowed to serve cake out of an army ration tin for dessert.

That night the rain continued and the next day as well. We were confined to our tents apart from our meals and visits to the now very unpleasant latrines. We dare not touch the top of our tent from the inside, as this would cause a leak. In the end we had three leaks adding to our discomfort. We mostly played cards. Mills always won but we did stop him smoking in the tent but he just sat by the door flap and blew the smoke out into the rain.

The Wednesday was our last full day. The weather had improved and had become showery. Our planned tasks for the day had been cancelled so it was another day in camp.

This time the NCOs had us lifting boulders from the stream and making a track for our lorry to get in from the road and out again when it came time to decamp and put all the equipment on board for the trip back to Essex.

First however we had to dig a trench round our tent just in case the stream that was now a raging torrent came over its banks and flooded us out. Whilst it had stopped raining the supply of water from the mountains still increased and this made the stream swell continuously.

The stream kept within its banks and the lorry never used the boulder road so we wasted a complete day but it kept us occupied.

On the Thursday we left for Fort William in the late afternoon to pick up the train to Glasgow. As we sat at the station waiting for our train, a sense of relief prevailed amongst us all, it was all over and we were going home to Mum and Dad. For me, it was of course the first time away from them. Horrible! Never again, but ...wait a minute, what an experience it really was! Character building it certainly was and the fact that it still means something today says a lot.

Anyway we eventually left for Glasgow. Once there a different train would take us south. Would this mean another horrendous journey with no sleep and a long stop over in the sidings at somewhere like

Crewe? We left Glasgow and our first stop was to be Edinburgh. Hang on a minute we thought, what is going on here? No one had told us we were going back down the east coast instead of the west, the way we had come up to Scotland. We could have got the night post train from Glasgow but someone had decided otherwise – a very telling decision, as it was to turn out.

It was now close to midnight and we all settled down to sleep where we could. This time it was a train with the tables so not easy to get into a luggage rack and our NCOs were told to ensure we left the train in a better state this time.

I slept on the floor in the central aisle. Occasionally a passenger would step over me but I rarely stirred. On one occasion I did need the toilet. On my way back we slowed down as we went through a station. I read the station sign "Stenhousemuir" – where the hell is that I thought to myself. Now hang on there's a football team on the Pools with that name. Where exactly is this town? We hadn't reached Edinburgh yet, as far as I knew. That name of Stenhousemuir stuck with me. Within a few weeks of being back home the TV's "Tonight" programme did a piece about Stenhousemuir Football Club and its financial plight. The club did survive. I found out more about it. They played in claret just like Chelmsford City and my beloved Burnley and from that day on until now they remained my "Scottish club".

All night the train rumbled on. Seward was exhausted and gave up on his number spotting. We all slept well. Were we heading for London? None of us was familiar with this line. By breakfast time it was light. We were given some sandwiches. Soon after that I again headed to the train's toilet.

Seated there I did the business and just as I finished the train came to a halt. I stood up and looked out of the small window. We were in Peterborough station. I did the necessary and pulled up my pants and trousers. Right in front of my nose was a sign that said "Do not flush the toilet whilst the train is in the station". Now I had a dilemma. Do I scatter my waste across the tracks so the good people of Peterborough could dissect my diet if they had a mind to or do I stay put? If I took the former option I would bet that a guard would be waiting for me outside the door and fine me on the spot!

I decided on the latter. The problem was the train did not move for nearly half an hour. Why? One could never know but I did have one of our group banging on the door and telling me to get out but I told him to go away and use another toilet, which he did.

I was getting tense by the second as we stayed there for what seemed ages. Eventually we moved off and I was able to flush at last.

Via Colchester we eventually got to Chelmsford. It was mid morning. At Chelmsford station our adventure had come to an end. Mum and Dad were not due back until the day after so I went back to Brian and Hazel's. My cousin was still struggling with her blood pressure. I tried to regale them with the stories from my adventure but, bless them, they were not, quite understandably, all that interested. Mum and Dad were the same when they got back – more interested in their holiday tales than hearing about mine.

Of course, it was not a holiday at all. I was homesick, tired, worn out and wish I'd never gone but then again what an experience, what character building, what a way to understand the different types of people we were.

Years further on we still remember the 1963 camp. I visited the site in 2008 and the boulder road we built is still there where we had camped. The place was desolate in that February and looked so different from that hot August of '63.

We certainly do remember the east coast journey back – for a start it was a lot quicker than the west coast journey we had had up to Scotland. However, had we caught that west coast train that evening, we could have been on the same train as that raided by the Great Train Robbers as it happened on the very same night we were travelling on the other line. Now that would have been a story!

What of the boys on that trip? Alan Mills left school at the end of the fifth year never to be heard of again.

Richard Green became an Accountant and "Stodge" Stoneham a Local Government Officer. We remain friends to this day and often talk about "that camp".

As for Chris Seward the story is a sad one. He gave up train spotting and made it to Oxford. Whilst later working for an International Aid Group he was hacked to death with a machete in the African bush by tribesmen. He was a good bloke and we all felt sad at his tragic end.

11

ONE STEP AHEAD!

Most of our teachers would wear their black gowns to normal lessons but some chose not to. When we had Speech Day they would all wear their gowns and they would include their "colours", a sort of shawl, showing which university they graduated from. The better looking the colour the more upmarket the university it seemed.

Take John Jordan for example. He was a fellow of Emmanuel College Cambridge and had this wonderful ermine type colour draped round his neck.

Even at a "dress up" event like Speech Day some teachers still did not have a gown to wear. Most were the PE teachers who perhaps had a diploma from a "Poly" instead of a degree and this would explain the lack of the gown.

There was one teacher however who never had a gown in our early years although he took General

Science classes for boys up to the Third Year. He was Mr Hale who carried the nickname of "Sparky" – he was not exceptional but good enough to take these classes in our early years. It seemed that he did most of his teaching from the course book but was able to refrain from anything elaborate such as chemical experiments as these did not appear on the curriculum until the Fourth Year. He did show us how to use a Bunsen burner and other similar basic tasks but that was all.

As we moved up the school and the men with the gowns took over the science lessons from "Sparky", rumours surfaced that he had at last got A-level Physics and Chemistry. This was comforting to those in the First, Second and Third Years but would still not impress those in the Fourth Year and above, who were by then studying for their O and A-Levels.

It was now widely rumoured that having got his A-levels he was now studying for a degree through something akin to the Open University, which was yet to make its mark in the educational world.

So another Speech Day came around and we noted there was still no gown for "Sparky". It seemed that it was as if he had to hide in the back row of the teachers as they sat behind the Head on the stage. There appeared to be a pecking order in where they all sat with the senior teachers in the front, including the Deputy Head, and then the heads of department and then it became a question of the university you attended – Oxbridge degrees took precedence it seemed in the seating plan to, say, Cardiff or Exeter! As he was small in stature, "Sparky" was almost invisible to the boys of the school seated in the Hall. He knew his place! He was the Ronnie Corbett character in the Cleese-Barker-Corbett sketch!

Two years on and Speech Day arrives. The Head leads in his masters. "Bruiser" Findlay immediately behind him, then "Tom" Bromwich, the tall and elegant "Noggs" Newman and then we nearly fainted with surprise it was "Sparky"! A beautiful very dark black gown (it was clearly new) and not the best of colours but colours nonetheless.

A degree! Well done, "Sparky", now you can come out of the back row and take your place in the "Ronnie Barker position" and look down on those with only their "Poly" degrees. You can take on the O-level syllabus for the Fourth and Fifth years and, who knows, in a couple of years the Head might let you deal with the A-level boys.

So, late in his career, "Sparky" Hale had reached his pinnacle. He probably had only a few years at the "top" as retirement could not have been that far away.

Now he teaches the rudiments of science to the angels and we just know he is proud of that gown which he wears in front of them and no longer does he have to hide away in the back row!

12

COULD I HAVE THE SIGHTSCREEN MOVED PLEASE?

Throughout the summer term the various school teams played matches against other Grammar schools in Essex. They were nearly always on Saturday afternoons and a coach would take two teams to another school whilst another two teams would play home matches against the same opposition.

On a particularly humid day in the summer of 1964 the Under 15s and the First XI were at Royal Liberty School in Romford. A coach picked up the team from the school and took us up the A12. We had two masters to accompany us and they spent the whole hour's journey swotting up on the copious Laws of Cricket, as they were forced to give up a Saturday each summer umpiring a game they often had little knowledge of. They knew about as much about cricket as I did about Greek verbs. Their normal idea on dealing with the lbw rule was to decline the first two appeals but then give the third whether the batsman was actually out or not.

We were Under 15s and had a decent team with the likes of Hughes, Sargent, Gunn, Ottley, Stoneham, Gurling, Cronin, Biddlecombe and the irrepressible Steve Cawley. The sky was beautifully blue when Royal Liberty batted. And batted. And batted. The First XI had a proper wicket to play on but we were on an artificial strip of bitumen. We had one of these at our own school but we did not play other schools on it. Our own one was lethal as it was laid out in blocks and the cracks were nearly two inches wide and if the ball landed on them you were fortunate to escape with your life, there being no helmets in those days for us to wear – we'd have a "box" if we were lucky!

Royal Liberty had no fears of their strip that still had the telltale cracks and racked up a score near to 200. Gunn's swing bowling, Cronin's pace and Stoneham's guile had little effect that day.

After tea we had our turn at batting. For once our star batsman and captain, Biddlecombe, soon had his wicket shattered - his normally immaculate defence breached by a ball keeping low off a crack. The stumps were an all in one unit on a metal base with the stumps on springs – the bitumen being too solid for conventional stumps. They made a dreadful clatter when hit. Wickets fell at regular intervals and our only hope of avoiding defeat was the weather. The blue skies had gone and there was a threat of a thunderstorm as the humidity rose.

With seven wickets down Cawley, a hard-hitting, strong batsman who could also bowl a lively medium pace joined me at the crease.

The first thing he said when we batsmen met mid wicket for a chat was "Look here, there's rain up there and if we can delay things as much as possible we might just be spared from a huge defeat. See that sightscreen over there I'm going to get it moved that'll waste some time, you watch me!"

Now the sightscreen was not the type normally seen at cricket grounds because, as the artificial strip meant that games were always played in the one place, the sightscreen did not have to be on wheels, or need to be moved at all, normally.

Royal Liberty, like most schools then and now, did not have a lot of money to spend on such fine things as sophisticated white screens to enable batsmen to see the ball better. They had put up a large white sheet about four times larger than one found on a bed and had tied it on halfway up the tall fencing built to stop cricket balls and footballs going into the adjacent gardens.

The sheet had seen better days and had a large split in it and flapped in the wind. Cawley politely asked their umpire if it could be moved as the split in it was right behind where the bowler's arm was when he delivered the ball and Cawley could not pick it up against the now blackening background, well at least that is what he claimed.

Being a decent chap and wanting to help the opposition, the umpire asked the boys from the fielding side to go to the fence and move it. Unfortunately for them the sheet was some fifteen feet or more off the ground. So as we batters waited forever glancing up at the threatening clouds that looked full of rain, a group of boys climbed up the fencing and undid the ropes holding the sheet in place and at Cawley's direction moved it so it was more precisely behind the bowler's arm without a gaping hole.

After more than twenty minutes the game recommenced, the sky was even darker but the better-positioned sheet made no difference as we both went the way of Biddlecombe. It didn't rain and we lost the match.

13

UNDER 15s ONLY

Football formed a large part of our lives at KEGS but more so in later years for most and in particular for me!

Those of us coming from such a large primary school as Kings Road had known nothing but success as we picked up the League and Cup double in our final year at the school in 1959/60 when we attained 11.

For me I had been on the fringe of the team having had a mysterious ankle injury in the summer of 1959 that necessitated my leg being put in plaster for six weeks. I was able to start the season of 1959-60 but only in the second team. I graduated to the first team by the end of the season. We had some excellent players such as Gus Gunn who was successful in the district trials and made the district side.

Once we got to the Grammar School our burgeoning football careers were put on hold as there was no under 12s team just under 13s so we were competing against second years for a place in the school team and they were of course a lot bigger than us. So I, like most of the first years, languished in limbo as far as football was concerned. I was even more upset about this as my parents had bought be a brand new pair of *adidas* football boots with their dashing white stripes and blue, yes blue, soles! The problem was that I hardly got any chance to wear them and within months my feet had grown too big for them. Even in our park matches with jumpers for goalposts I could not wear them as we all had to wear either boots or just our old shoes and we all had to wear the same. As some lads had no boots it was shoes for all!

By the time the second year came round we all went for the under 13s' trials. I failed to get selected and that was it for the under 14s and 15s -once you were in you were in and once you were out you were out! I remember the football master for some of that time was a Mr Clark. For what I thought was no apparent reason he did not like me that much and also taught me Latin for a short while. At one parent–teachers meeting my Dad nearly decked him over what Mr Clark said about me as a person. Yes I was useless at Latin but he told my Dad I was a bit of a big head! Now, quite a few years on many might say he was right! However, my Dad took exception to the way the comment was phrased and many who knew my Dad would say that he was the most kind and gentle man you could ever meet and so whatever Clark said, or how he said it, must have been pretty bad.

Interestingly the next time Clark wrote on my school report he said and I quote, "Has tried hard in a quiet sort of way" – he clearly recalled how he had upset my Dad but I still didn't get picked for the school team!

So in the autumn of 1963 I was 14 and spent my Saturdays following the exploits of Chelmsford City with other non-players like "Stodge" Stoneham, "Froggy" Frost and the older Roger Bird and Mick Newman.

During the week though I would long to get into the school teams but when we had Games lessons the Under 15s would have their own group for "Under 15s only" and the rest of us would just have to feel jealous!

A year later we would be under 16s but there was no team at that age and we just had the First and Second XIs. So, you were now up against older boys and the competition was stiff so hardly any of our year got a game until they got into the sixth form in 1965

For me the only football available at that time was to go training with my Dad at a school not far from where we lived. My Dad who was then in his mid-forties took the training sessions for the team from the factory where he worked, Christy's. The team called, Christy's Sports, played in one of the lower divisions of the Chelmsford and Mid Essex league where teams were full of a mix of non-achievers in the football world who just loved playing or young kids like me. At 14 I was too young to play in that football.

From the age of 13 I did turn out for Oaklands United who played Saturday morning football in the Chelmsford Junior League, which was under 15s. Of course, only those from our school not in the school teams played in this as most school games were on Saturdays. So "Stodge" and I joined Oaklands through our friends Terry Ketley and Vince Bramhall. It was a tough baptism as we were slight 13 year olds up against strapping 15 year olds. We were not a great team but not quite the worst in our League.

As I gradually got a little bigger I was able to cope with training with the men of Christy's in the gym on Wednesday evenings. I was now, in the winter of 1964-65, too old for the junior league and not good enough for the school.

One Saturday lunchtime I was eating my dinner when a car pulled up outside the house and one of the Christy's lads got out and came to the door. My Dad, fortunately, had just arrived home from his normal Saturday morning at the factory. The team were one short for the afternoon's match and would Dad let me play? He left it up to me and I went and got my boots and left with the Christy's man!

Off we went to our "home" ground Melbourne Park where there were the usual 15 pitches and we normally played on one of the muddiest. I cannot recall the result but I did all right despite an attack of cramp towards the end of the game. The other players thought I was good for a 15 year old and I thought that they should tell the school selectors that!

So at the age of 15 I was on the football map at last. Being speedy but still a little weedy meant I could skip round the cloggers unless they were good enough to scythe me down, which they frequently did. It was a tough grounding as a lot of these players knew the tricks of the football trade so that you could get the **ball** past them or **you** could get past them but **you and the ball** getting past together was not quite so easy!

The school season ended at Christmas and a few of the team came and played in local football. Some turned out for the Old Chelmsfordians who ran six Saturday teams and were always looking to encourage young boys to come along and enjoy their football and then some socialising in their bar afterwards. It was not until I was 17 that I started playing for them on Sunday mornings.

For me it was Christy's when I was just 15. I recall my first goal and, in fact, still have the newspaper cutting about it. It was a diving header on a snowy pitch against Great Leighs, a village a few miles out of Chelmsford, in a 2-1 win. I have to confess that even as an innocent looking 15 year old there was an element of the "Hand of God" about this goal long before Maradona invented it! I had my fist next to the left side of my head and as the ball brushed my forehead it took a big deflection off my fist and into the goal. Not a soul noticed!

Into the second part of the season and into 1965, we were a mid table team and the runaway leaders were H.M. Prison! They had dispensation from the Home Office to play in the local league and got plenty of coverage in the National Press! They had two advantages; one was that they played all their games at home (obviously!) and the other that they could train all week!

Chelmsford Prison was a dark foreboding place on the inside with a pitch right in the middle of the buildings. At training on the Wednesday the Christy's lads had told me that, if asked, I was to say I was 16 as it was unlawful to go inside a prison if you were under that age! I was also warned that there would be a big crowd of prisoners watching and they would have large bets (with cigarettes normally) on certain aspects of the match – i.e. margin of victory etc. They would be vociferous and might pick on me, being a bit lightweight.

It was a dank February day when our team arrived at the prison gates. Taken inside we were counted. We went through a whole series of doors and were counted each time, as if we would run away and hide in a place like that! As expected the PT Instructor in charge of the team strode over to us and told us some of the rules like no conversation with or passing anything to the opposition all of whom were prisoners, no staff were allowed to play. Our manager had brought a few cigarettes and would make sure these were passed on to the prisoners away from the gaze of the PTI or the warders. The PTI came right up to me and said gruffly, "How old are you son?" In the same way as Mr Mackay would in Porridge! I answered weakly, "Sixteen sir" – I am sure he did not believe me but let it go.

We got changed and being continuously counted made our way to the pitch. It was raining outside so the crowd was well down on the norm and the pitch was muddy. We lost 5-1 but there were some interesting occurrences. Their captain for the day had been our captain the season before, and that doesn't happen very often! Jock had been done for receiving stolen goods and got a one-year stretch!

In the opening few minutes I had a shot from about 25 yards and it nearly went over the prison wall, cue catcalls from those prisoners around the touchline. I looked sheepish and embarrassed!

We were 2-0 down at half time and in our team talk at half time we said one quick goal in the second half and we'd be back in it.

Almost immediately after the restart, I was played through on goal chased by a defender, it was the chance we had looked for but the keeper came out, dived at my feet and smothered the ball away.

As we trooped into the changing room muddied and beaten at the end of the game I apologised to the team for missing that great chance especially as I was clean through with just this goalie to beat. Don't worry, I was told, the goalkeeper's in for manslaughter and all my teammates agreed that they, too, would have let him get to the ball first!

I was told not to have a shower by my mates who formed a protective ring round me in the changing room. The reason I subsequently found out was that some of the "trusties" would come round offering soap and towels and their "cleaning" services. They were as camp as they come and clearly my mates saw me as a vulnerable target – a virgin I suppose!

So all this was great character building and as time went on it developed me physically and mentally to play in youth football so much so that by the autumn of 1966 I was in the school first XI. I had caught up with my peers including some of the Kings Road team.

That school team of 1966 has its photo adorning the walls of the clubhouse of the Old Chelmsfordians' Association and in the school archives and my own school memory album.

For some reason it has become an iconic picture of that age. It was probably the first where the team had modern and trendy hair styles and the kit was of the time where it all looked mostly the same as opposed to a motley collection of cast offs and second hand stuff of varying shades of red and black that had been seen in the years before.

Back Row: Gurling, Burton, Smith, Roberts, Biddlecombe
Front Row: Little, Flint, Gunn, Hughes, Hollebon, Cole

The pen pictures of the team with its details updated are: -

Dick Smith – goalkeeper – in the Gordon Banks mould at the time – big, strong and capable – picked for Essex Senior Schools in 1967-68. Became Primary School Headmaster.

Paul Biddlecombe – elegant centre half who insisted that we all had those haircuts in the mod tradition and looked "hard" and unsmiling in the team photo. Senior figure in Motor and other industries and in many sports clubs.

Ian "Gus" Gunn – as mentioned before, named after Gorgeous Gus in the comics because of his hard shot. Captain of this team and always led well by example in the Bobby Moore mould. Senior Engineer for W S Atkins.

Simon Hughes – midfield – elegant called "stroller" for his laid back approach on the field. One of those annoying people who were both brainy and good at all sports. Prefect's Room Shove Halfpenny champion! Chief Executive of Mothercare.

Tim Burton – stylish winger with the withering Frank Lampard like looks that made the girl's swoon. Architect.

Jack Gurling – no prisoners taken type of midfielder in the Nobby Stiles mould. Teacher.

Peter Hollebon – young right winger with immaculate hairstyle and quite literally a nose for goal! Legal profession then Financial Adviser.

Paul Roberts – sulky but silky like Rooney – played in the "hole" and scored many vital goals in the way that Martin Peters did at the time. Stockbroking and other areas of the financial world. Sadly died in early middle age.

Chris Flint – new "signing" that summer from Norfolk (his dad changed jobs and moved!) – striker. Banking and Accountancy world.

Dave Cole – left footed full back or left midfield, quick and incisive but had no school black and red socks that day! Local Government.

Me – first game for the school was left back and the next as a right-winger! Eventually settled as a striker – Financial world and now trying to write!

Apart from Paul who died a few years ago the team is still in some form of contact with each other! Quite remarkable!

14

RAIN STOPPED PLAY! OR HAS IT?

School holidays were mostly a welcome delight in our years at KEGS. However, in the later years we had to do revision for exams or catch up on work but in our early years we were free to do what we liked.

For us it was football in the winter and cricket and football through the summer. Terry and Rob Ketley living just around the corner would be constant companions along with many other schoolmates who would join us at the local parks. There could be a dozen or more of us at times.

Inevitably, rain would stop play at any time of the year as well as the ice and snow in the winter.

So what then? With the Ketleys nearby and Neil Ritchie over the road and a few others not far away we would meet at someone's house and play indoor games. There was very little daytime TV and the radio was boring so we had to make our own entertainment. Terry Ketley was our leader and would invent all sorts of games with younger brother Rob. One was a cricket game involving an empty cardboard shoebox with little rectangles cut out of the long side. These cut outs were of different size and the object was to roll a marble from about a yard away through the holes and into the box – the largest hole was a "one" and the smallest a "six". Three misses and you were out. So using this you could have a full cricket match and we often set out to complete one. It would take hours but then we had hours.

Unfortunately the matches often did not reach a conclusion as the rain stopped and we went outside and resumed the football or cricket matches suspended due to the weather.

Sometimes we would turn on the TV in the afternoons and watch the horse racing. Terry and Rob did not have a TV so they would come round to mine to watch it and two or three others might join us.

To while away an hour or two as the rain continued to fall, we would have individual bets on each race. Not with money as we had none but with McVitie's digestive biscuits! I would be allowed by Mum to offer one to each friend and we would then break up each biscuit into, say, six pieces. We would bet one piece on the horses in each race. The winner takes all and can eat the winnings.

So as each race came we nominated one or two horses depending on the size of the field.

The betting would come up and the first time we ever did this we were soon to show our naivety. The betting show was something like this: -

2/1 Devil's Advocate
100/30 Runner's Mate
5/1 Prince Charming
8/1 Shining Star
10/1 Bar

We all chose a horse and these were recorded. Terry Ketley chose the lightly fancied "Bar" at 10/1. As the race unfolded Terry was bemused that his horse did not get a mention and demanded a mini steward's enquiry, which was rejected by us all.

When the next race was being discussed and the early show of betting came up on the screen, Terry soon noticed that "Bar" was actually in this race and was at the bottom of the betting at 20/1. He bet his next section of digestive and assumed the BBC had made an error by putting the horse in the wrong race details.

Again, as the horses completed their six furlongs he was more than a little annoyed that "Bar" still did not get a mention. He was apoplectic and was almost on the point of writing a letter of complaint except he would not really know who to send it to!

The next race information came up and unbelievably in the first show of betting "Bar" was in this race too. This time we all sat and listened to what Peter O'Sullevan had to say about the runners and riders. No "Bar" was mentioned as each horse was shown in turn then Mr O'Sullevan went through the latest betting and this time said 12/1 …bar those five. Suddenly it dawned on us what "Bar" actually meant. Cue hysterical laughter and even Terry joined in although a little embarrassed, like the rest of us really!

15

CHEATS NEVER PROSPER, OR DO THEY!?

When we sat our Mock O-levels in February 1965 "Tired of Waiting For You" by the Kinks was Number One in the charts but I just could not concentrate on my revision so, of the nine Mocks that I sat, I passed just two and if I repeated this in the real thing in the summer it would not get me a place in the sixth form (five minimum was required and after a terrific fourth academic year at school my fifth would be my disappointing last!).

Anyway back in the February I was struggling. I was tired and a bit depressed and my schoolwork was not as it should have been and then we had these blasted Mocks. The amount of revision was immense and these were only a "trial run" I kept telling myself. Peak in July not February was my mantra but, hang on, if I performed too badly I would not be put in for the real thing. Pressure! I could not handle it.

I managed to convince my Mum and Dad that the Chinese meal out of a packet had done for me so I could not possibly sit Geography – a vast subject that I had not prepared properly for, yet it was one of my favourites and one that I wanted to take at A-level.

Chemistry was a complete mystery to me. For O-level I had wanted to do Physics but if I did that subject I would have to drop one of my favourite "Arts" subjects in favour of doing a more "Science" orientated block of subjects – that was how the system worked. So I did Chemistry as my ninth O-level subject through necessity rather than choice.

Before the Chemistry Mock I had a ruse that if I took a piece of paper into the exam in my pocket with important chemical formulae on it then I could mix it with the papers on the desk and refer to it as required.

It was easy to get the right type of paper, just walk out with a piece from the previous day's exam. Surely, in a hall of 100 boys no one will see me add this sheet to the many pieces already on the desk in the exam hall?

Just as we were at registration in our classrooms I suddenly felt giddy and couldn't focus at all. I felt queasy and my hands were cold but I was sweating profusely. I was to have these symptoms again during my adult life and they are a form of migraine, apparently, probably on this occasion brought on by the stress or a penance for preparing to cheat!

On this day I got through the exam despite feeling pretty ill. I did get the piece of paper out of my pocket and got away with adding it to the other pieces on the desk. I even used some of what was on there. Did it help? No!

I failed the Mock and the real O'-level in the summer and felt that someone had taught me a lesson!

...

Lost and found

After more than 40 years it's time to come clean and get things off my chest!

We all bend the rules and we all try to get away with things but we all do good deeds as if trying to compensate in some way. Even when we do that we sometimes let ourselves down!

Take Steve Robbins and me. We left the school's annexe at Friars School to cycle home for our dinner when right outside the school and in the road was a £1 note. We gathered it up and decided to detour to the police station to hand it in. Mad you might think but £1 would buy you a lot in 1962 especially if you consider that a litre of petrol was about 6p so the £1 is near to £20 today. If this happened nowadays we'd all look round say thank you very much and put it in our pockets. Not so we two!

The desk sergeant at the police station complimented us on our honesty but looked at us as if we were completely mad but said that if the note is not claimed within a month they would write to me and we could call in and collect it.

We both forgot about it until I received a letter from the police saying that no one had claimed the note so it was mine (actually of course mine and Steve's). He had clearly forgotten about the whole incident and had never mentioned it again. Shamefully, I kept the £1 for myself! Sadly, Steve is no longer with us but if he were I would gladly give him the current day equivalent of ten bob. Steve, if you're up there I'll pay you when I see you.

...

Don't trust your mates!

I was pretty useless at Maths and was in Set 3 of 4 based on ability and that was being generous to me! Andy Lemon was a mate and should really have been in Set 1 or 2. Mr Pettit was our teacher and very much a "character" in the staff room. He was a pretty good teacher but I was just useless at anything analytical like algebra and geometry. I was good at mental arithmetic and such like but to get O-level Maths, which was a must for everyone, you needed a good all round ability at the subject. Failure to get the O-level, we were told, would mean we could never go to university or even get a job, well not one we would want anyway!

The O-levels were a little way off and maybe I could sneak a pass with just my mental arithmetic, which formed the first part of the O-level paper. So one day we had this test that included some complex, to me at least, calculations. The classrooms were the classic designs of the time that of neat rows of desks. Andy Lemon sat to my right and wrote furiously away as if he knew exactly what he was doing. I looked at Mr Pettit and he was busy at his desk marking books from a previous class. I moved closer to Lemon with my chair. Now I'd recently gone to wearing glasses for short sightedness so my 20/20 vision helped me see exactly what the maths star Lemon had done. I changed my layout from his but the page long calculation and answer looked very similar to Lemon's. I knew that with a correct calculation the working would look very similar from one person to another in Maths unlike copying text so it would not look quite as suspicious. We handed in our papers.

At the next Maths lesson, Mr Pettit took me to one side and showed me my answer and Lemon's; they were remarkably similar but the trouble was the trusty Lemon had made a complete pig's ear of his calculation and I, more like a sheep than a pig, had followed exactly.

Mr P knew it was no coincidence and seeing I was banged to rights I soon owned up. Mr P could have taken action himself but passed the buck to my form master W R "Jake" Jackson.

After school and a cricket match I had to go and see him in his apartment in the Boarding House at about 7pm. He was an affable chap and was still in his 20s so knew all about the wiles of the schoolboy as he had been one only a short time before. He told me off but what happened next was that we got into a philosophical discussion on cheating, modern behaviour and this went on for about an hour. Being fifteen or sixteen at the time I was full of myself and had opinions about everything. "Jake" liked me, I think, as I had been a good History pupil and had just had my one good academic year on most subjects, which he knew all about as being my form master he wrote general comments at the end of my school report. Even before our discussion he had given me the option of the slipper or a hundred lines. I had opted for the slipper to get it over with, which probably was not what he was expecting. Anyway he let me off and told me to remember, "Cheats never prosper". I did manage to get maths O-level by the skin of my teeth getting a grade 6, when 7, 8 and 9 were "Fails".

...

Caught but not really

Since I was about four I had known Steve Cawley. His Dad, Tom, and my Dad, Norman, had worked at Christy's in Chelmsford together for many years and played cricket together for the firm's team. So, for many Saturday's in the summer Steve and I would be with our Dads at the matches invariably at either of the two council owned pitches in Admiral's Park. We would watch a bit of the cricket for all of two minutes then we'd be off playing in the woods near the pitch or back in the play area in the park where there were swings, a carousel on which to make yourself ill, a rocking horse contraption with six seats and as large a slide as you could imagine and, oh yes, a shallow river to mess about in.

We were barely of school age when we would spend hours playing there – a far cry from what young kids do today. At about 4.45 the Christy's van would appear with its driver and my Mum who had done the cricketer's teas back at the canteen at the "Works", as it was always referred to. Tea was at 5 and Steve and I would run back and enjoy the most wonderful sandwiches, easily the best compared with any of the clubs where our Dads played. The cups of tea were so refreshing and delivered from the urn brought down from the "Works". Mum would go back with the driver to wash up and he would drop her back at the cricket just before close but in time for us all to adjourn to the Black Bull for a well earned drink.

There we would enjoy orange squash (a ginger beer if we were lucky -perhaps if Christy's had won!) and a packet of crisps with their little blue packet of salt – there would be only one flavour available in those days.

Steve C would stay for a while but then he and Tom would have to catch their bus to Roxwell some miles away.

So we had been together for about six hours and being kids were always arguing, vying to be the best and falling out. Steve was nearly nine months older than me and a lot bigger (he still is!) but whilst he was always wiser than me he never used the advantage of his physical strength to gain one up on me but invariably managed it anyway. So we had this sort of love-hate relationship.

Each year up to about the age of ten we would go the kid's Christmas/New Year party put on by Christy's where we would sit in the canteen at long tables and have a meal, normally a salad. Steve and I would be together often trying to work out how Father Christmas bothered to turn up here half way through January when he must be tired out and really due a holiday! After the tea we would watch the magician, sing some songs and then get our presents from Father Christmas who wore glasses just like those of Jim Weller who worked with our Dads.

In the school holidays Steve would cycle over to where I lived and with other school friends we would play cricket and football. For some reason we two often niggled at each other. It was probably my fault, as he always seemed better than me, being that much older. Amazingly, he would cycle home for his dinner and back again. It was a five mile journey so he often cycled twenty miles a day just to play with us! Why did he not bring sandwiches? Why did one of us not offer him some dinner? It is difficult to understand now.

When we were about 11 I had a serious injury to my knee whilst on holiday in Jersey. I fell and cut open my kneecap. So deep and wide was the cut that the hospital could not stitch it. That was in early August and by early September it was healing nicely with a scab. One day we were playing football in the park with our Frido ball and I went past Steve in a dribble. He was getting to the age when a few players did that to him and he had seen enough tackling down at Chelmsford City matches to know how to execute the Peter Gillott (City's awesome full back) famous late tackle. Over I went right on my knee. The ground was hard and the scab sliced off as neat as you like – blood poured out. I started to cry and got up and whacked Steve right in the solar plexus, a definite red card if there had been such a thing but, then, he might have been sent off as well. I was taken by Anne Cornwall, who was on the swings nearby, round to her Nan's who bathed it and stuck a peculiar green plaster on it. My relationship with Steve was soured; well at least from my point of view, for about a year.

In May the following year we were on the field next to the school playing cricket on the bitumen all weather wicket mentioned already. It was as bouncy and lethal as you like with its cracks and high bounce that would sometimes nearly take off your helmetless head.

Anyway I'm bowling and Steve's batting during this games lesson. The master is umpiring. Never being much of a bowler I fed Steve with a half volley which he hit straight back at me. It hit me in the midriff and my two hands came together to effect the caught and bowled. So ferocious was the hit that the ball dropped from my midriff bounced on the bitumen and went straight back into my hands. Great catch everyone shouted because Steve's was a prize scalp indeed. I immediately looked a bit sheepish and turned to say to the master that it was a "bump ball" but as I turned to look at him with Steve already walking off I remembered the scab and the blood and how it took me another month to nurture another scab. So, I kept my mouth shut.

Steve and I remain good friends to this day but maybe not once he knows the truth!

...

Gooseberries? We love them!

It is June 1965, Sandi Shaw is Number One in the charts with "Long Live Love" and our O-levels are due within a fortnight. Biology was an interesting and varied subject. Our text books covered all sorts of subjects and towards the end of it there was a long section about "Reproduction" – it dealt, briefly, with humans but all the definitions and diagrams were of rabbits which, when one thinks about it, is appropriate in view of their breeding habits! We never did get to cover this part of the book and whilst our

Steve Little

teacher never said anything about it he knew that the Oxford and Cambridge Examining Board would NEVER ask teenage boys and girls questions about reproduction!

Our teacher was Mr Underhay or "Pinhead" as we called him as he was very tall and had a small head. He was a decent teacher but not that friendly with us as some of the others were but he managed to get most of his charges through the O-level and none of us gave him a hard time in class.

Now this success may have been down to his teaching or maybe the fact that he effected a dramatic piece of cheating, sort of! With the O-levels so close the school would have already received certain information and requests from the examiners. Now, there was a practical section to Biology when we were given a flower or a fruit or a vegetable and had to dissect it in half, draw it onto our answer paper and name all the constituent parts. The school would have to know what that item was to be, as they would need to buy a large supply from the local market.

We were in the classroom waiting for "Pinhead" and he strode in and we stood up, as we always had to do when a master came into the room. He told us to sit down and he picked up a piece of chalk and went to the blackboard. "Now listen boys, I want you all to know how to spell this word." He wrote:

G O O S E B E R R Y

We all wrote it down. Why? We were not sure at first. Then one of us looked at another knowingly – nods passed around the room. Some boys looked and remained perplexed and had to be talked to after the lesson. What we told them was we need to know how to spell it, as we need to cut it in half, dissect it and name it in the forthcoming exam! Well, surprise, surprise examination day comes and the fruit to be dissected in the Biology exam is... a GOOSEBERRY!

Thank you Mr Underhay, we'll keep it as our secret!

Steve Little

16

MAKE SURE YOU CONCENTRATE DURING FRENCH REPRODUCTION!

Although most of the O-levels started in the first week of July some of the practical elements took place during June.

One such was part of the French examination. Many of us found it difficult to understand why we had to do French in the first place. Yes they were our nearest non-British neighbours but we were always falling out with them. At the time, President De Gaulle was famously saying "Non" to us joining the then equivalent of the EEC and to think that we gave him back his country in 1945! We supposed there was always a chance that they would give in when someone threatened them again and we would have to go over there and save them for the third time and then there was always the chance that a new Napoleon would appear, threatening our shores, and we would have to go to war with them for the umpteenth time! So this, presumably, was why we had to learn French so we would be able to converse with them!

Still French was quite easy to learn compared with Latin, which remained a daunting subject for us all.

German was only just getting into the schools bearing in mind the War had ended only about twenty years before and the wounds were still there. The Chinese were still a sleeping giant and there was no one to teach Mandarin anyway. We already spoke refined American so, at the end of it all, French was deemed the most appropriate foreign language for us to learn.

There were four parts to French O-level. There was the normal paper that we would sit in July, which would be French into English and English into French. In June though we had "Dictee" and what was amusingly called "French Reproduction". As we often had attractive French ladies over here for a spell as a "French Assistant", there were plenty of we sixteen year olds who would like a bit of French Reproduction with these ladies but this was only in our dreams!

"Dictee" and "French Reproduction" was where we were examined in our normal classrooms. "Dictee" was where the teacher read out sentences in French and we had to write them out word for word in French. For "French Reproduction" the teacher would read us a story in French and then we would have to re-write the story in French in our own words. We were kindly given some French phrases from the story to help us put together a passable version of what we had just heard. We had done these countless times in practice but then the marks did not matter too much but now it was different.

The "Dictee" was fairly easy. Now came the more daunting story we had to reproduce.

Now, in June the warmth in the classrooms was considerable and on this particular day it was also a warm day outside. The classroom overlooked our upper playground and as we listened to the story I noticed a group of boys playing five a side football out there and as the master droned on with the story my eyes wandered so I was looking out of the window at the game unfolding in the playground. I suddenly realised that I had now missed a good five minutes of the story. Now this would have been fine in a normal lesson but this was the O-level for goodness sake!

I concentrated hard on the rest of the story and I thought I could rely on the prompts to help me with the reproduction. The story was a little complicated; it was something to do with two sisters separately going to a dance but one was dressed as a young man and her sister became interested in her/him and I was as confused as the young lady. I recalled Shakespeare wrote a play with the same sort of story and I desperately tried to remember how that turned out because my lapse in concentration had meant that I really missed the middle part of the French story so it made the understanding of the ending more difficult. I could not recall what Shakespeare's ending was either so that did not help so I just had to guess.

I guessed wrongly as I found out from my friends when we got outside the classroom when the exam ended. Not a good start to getting French O-level!

I would have to rely on my normally inadequate written exam to get through but before that there was always "French Conversation" which was the third part of this O-level.

All the boys taking French would one by one be called into a room to have a five-minute conversation in French. Typical of our school days everything was done in strict alphabetical order so at least I was half way down the order so could quiz quite a few of my friends to see what sort of areas the examiners would cover. Not that this would make all that much difference to me!

I was pretty useless at any previous attempts at conversational French and had at that time never been across the Channel. Galling was the fact that my Dad spoke fluent vernacular French as he had been billeted with a French speaking family in Algiers during the War and was with them for a year. He never offered his help but then I never sought it. As teenagers then (and now probably) we did not ever wish to show any sort of weakness in front of our Dads!

Anyway my time with the examiners was due. I knocked hesitantly on the door of the room and was called in by the examiner, in French. There sat a genial man and a more severe looking woman who said nothing until "au revoir" at the end but she wrote things down on her pad throughout.

"Comment allez-vous?"

"Je vais bien," I said confidently (I was well prepared for this start!).

"Comment vous appelez-vous?"

"Je m'appelle Little." This is so easy but then I knew exactly what they were going to ask and what my response would be.

I was asked to sit down and managed a "Merci" I was even impressing myself with my start!

The next question, the French for which now escapes me, was asking what I was doing during the summer holidays. Now, I was off to Northern Italy with my parents so I answered that I was going to Italy.

Where in Italy came the question. I took a few seconds to translate in my brain what the man had asked and then flushed as I forgot the French for

North (more than a little disappointing as Nord is not too dissimilar from North!) so I said "Le Sud".

Where in the "Le Sud" came the response. I hesitated. Where the hell was I likely to go to in the South? Fortunately "Noggs" Newman's thoroughness at teaching us Geography meant I knew Naples was somewhere down towards the heel of Italy so "Naples" was my answer.

This was all becoming a little more comfortable now as some of these words were, of course, the same or similar in French as in English. It got even better when I was asked what my hobbies were. Again my friends had primed me with this as a likely question as they had all been asked it before my turn had come around.

"Le football, le cricket, le pop music," – Wow, dazzling "French"!

"What type of pop music do you like?" was the immediate response.

"Les Beatles, Les Rolling Stones, Les Kinks, and the equally impressive, Les Mamas and Papas (but the latter at least had three possible words used in France!). The body language of the examiner suggested I was doing well. Perhaps it had been a long day already for him and he had not really noticed that more than half my French oral exam was, in fact, being conducted in English or at best a form of Franglais!

The session soon ended and I knew I'd impressed them.

I secured my O-level (Grade 5) and I put it down to that weird French oral when I was near faultless with my Franglais!

17

WHAT TIME IS THE LAST TRAIN TO CHELMSFORD?

It's that week between Christmas and New Year 1965/1966. Snow fell on Boxing Day and the ground was covered in two or three inches and the temperatures remained at or below freezing and there was no thaw in sight.

We were now in the Lower Sixth and it was a year for a bit of fun. O-levels were behind us and A-levels were not until the summer of '67 for most of us.

One of our number had met some girls at a party before Christmas and one of them had invited him and some of his friends to a party at her parent's house immediately after Christmas.

None of us was old enough to drive then so we had to rely on public transport – there were no parents with 4x4s in those days to ferry us around and in fact many did not have a car at all.

The problem with the party was that it was on a Sunday night. Not something that was common in those days. The other problem was that it was being held in Shenfield some ten miles away from Chelmsford or two train stops on the upline to Liverpool Street. With the snow on the ground we had no option but to go by train, as buses were few and far between and anyway the last bus would be leaving Shenfield at about 10 p.m. We all had bikes but it was a bit too far in these wintry conditions and was not very groovy to turn up at a party on one!

Simon was in charge of organising the journey and about six of us turned up at about 7 p.m. at Chelmsford station to make the short trip up the line.

The young lady hostess lived about half a mile from Shenfield station in a very smart house in a private road.

These were no Internet fuelled raves with hundreds from all over turning up. These were sedate, quiet affairs often with parents in attendance in the next room and the guest list normally by strict invitation. Five of us did not know the girls but Simon had ensured that our group excluded those most likely to cause offence by downing too much alcohol. Some other local lads, who we did not know, were there already.

The party took on the norm with more boys there than girls. The rest of the procedure for the evening would follow a familiar pattern. There would be the initial chat between us all and a little sizing up of boy and girl. The parent's lounge would always have the large furniture removed but a settee and armchair would normally remain with other chairs situated around the walls. Expensive pots and ornaments would have been removed to the safety of the garage. One small table remained and on it would be the Dansette record player and a pile of 45s and the odd LP. The room would be too bright early on but fine for circling the group of girls and eying them up. Thankfully there was some decent music around at that time. That week "Daytripper/We Can Work It Out" a double A side was number one in the charts and our hostess had received the LP containing these for Christmas. To get things going she had the Beatles on and that was good for listening to. Then this was followed by the Rolling Stones latest LP that had their recent hits "Satisfaction" and "Get Off My Cloud" on it – this and a bit of the Kinks or similar would get a few dancing their version of a modified slow twist. Ken Dodd's recent "Tears", "The Carnival Is Over" by the Seekers and the classic "You've Lost That Loving Feeling" by the Righteous Brothers would be saved for later when smooching and a little groping would start as the bright lights were switched off and the subtle table lamp by the french windows turned on. This would create just enough light to enable us to see what we were stroking.

The early circling had evolved into a pairing off exercise. Those of us a little less forthright would then, partnerless, adjourn to the kitchen and talk about football and how crap the party was. The drink would be on the draining board. There would be a limit to the amount of alcohol and, once Gus was into it, it would soon be gone. The rest of us hoped he would get off early with one of the girls so it would leave more of the beer for us. This was the early days of Party Five and two of these did not stretch too far so we were soon on the lemonade.

Hostess's Mum had thoughtfully provided some pineapple chunks and cheese on sticks, some crisps, a few sausage rolls left over from Christmas and some mince pies made in early December and now a bit stale. These were never touched as mince pie and Watney's bitter was very much an acquired taste!

Occasionally one of the lads would come back into the kitchen having been cast aside by the girl. She would sit in the main room on one of the seats around the walls for a few minutes before a different lad would exit the kitchen to go and ask her for a smooch. There was a certain pecking order in this and it was as if an invisible queue existed.

Some times two lads would come back together as their two dance partners would have exchanged those secretive glances that only girls have where they can convey their message without opening their mouths!

By about 9.30 the whole thing had settled down. The queue had been exhausted and all substitutions made. The Righteous Brothers were doing their stuff and the table lamp had now been turned off. There would then be no dancing. The lucky two couples that got the settee and armchair would make the most of their good fortune. The other couples would have to make do with the more uncomfortable dining room chairs with the girl sitting on the boy's lap. Fortunately there was rarely a plump girl around in those days so the boys were more than likely able to cope with this weight on their thighs and probably enjoy it!

Those of us in the kitchen would still bemoan how crap the party had become and how we would really like to go home and watch the end of the evening's TV but as our mates were still in the dark room we must stick together and leave at 11.15 to catch the last train to Chelmsford.

On this particular night, the table lamp eventually went on to allow for the exchange of addresses and phone numbers to take place. Mum and Dad appeared and the full bright lights went on. Dad distributed the coats and we left. Those of us from the kitchen stood in the cold at the garden gate whilst the lucky boys said their final goodbyes in the porch.

We had to jog down to the station as the goodbyes had made things a little tight to get the 11.30. When the six of us arrived at the station we could see the stationmaster pulling the folding iron gate across the entrance, having already turned off the ticket hall lights.

Simon enquired of him, "What time is the last train to Chelmsford?"

"At 11.12," came the reply.

"But the timetable says 11.30, I checked it earlier," said Simon.

"Ah, you see, that's on a Saturday but today is Sunday and it's 11.12 on Sundays," the man answered in that sort of triumphant way these types of people use on such occasions.

Simon almost started to argue but thought better of it. He turned to us trying to find an excuse.

What do we do now was the consensus? Some could club together what they had in their pockets and get as near to Chelmsford as possible by taxi and then walk the rest.

Gus and I had nothing left in our pockets and opted to hitch. Having told Simon what a stupid arse he was we left the others and set off.

The snow was certainly deep and crisp and even by the side of the road and there was still compacted snow across the road. Not many cars were about. Not many people had cars anyway in 1965 and those that did would certainly not venture out on a freezing late December night.

The two of us had to walk about two miles along what had been the old A12 road before we got to the new A12 at the end of the Shenfield/Brentwood bypass and it was not until we got there that we even saw a car.

If Gus had had a few beers too many the cold soon sobered him up and he got a little concerned about the lack of likely lifts and it was all doom and gloom for a while.

Eventually an old Morris 1000 came into view with its traditional split windscreen. The driver had clearly not heard of de-icer and there were two little holes in the frosty screen for him to see through.

We eagerly thumbed at him. He slowed down and slid into the snowy slush by the side of the road and wound down the passenger side window, "I'm going to Galleywood, is that any help?"

Gus and I looked at each other and immediately nodded in agreement. "Great thanks," I said to the young man. Gus got in the front and I got in the back. Straightaway we had to get out again as the man could not get his wheels out of the pile of snow he had stopped in, so we had to give him a push into the middle of the road.

Now Galleywood was on the Shenfield side south of Chelmsford so quite a way from Broomfield where we lived and that is north of Chelmsford. We didn't mind though as we could walk the last three miles.

The driver was not that much older than us and was a university student on his way back to his parents having spent Christmas with his girlfriend's parents.

He dropped us off near the Britvic factory south of Chelmsford and we got home at about 1.30. We had phoned home before we left Shenfield to tell our parents our plight so they would not be that worried when we arrived much later than expected.

The others got home OK but Simon was "persona non grata" with us for a while. He was destined to become our Head Boy, get a top degree from London and become a senior executive with such illustrious companies as BHS, Mothercare and Somerfield but as for reading a straightforward rail timetable…?

18

"THIS IS THE ONLY WAY WE'LL EVER GET TO CAMBRIDGE! HOWEVER, WE COULD END UP AT THE OLD BAILEY!"

In order to be allowed into the sixth form you needed to pass at least five O-levels. Those who got four or less may have left the school at the end of the fifth year or did re-sits in the autumn term after the exams having spent the time in what was called "The Remove" which was a state of limbo between the fifth and sixth years.

So we sixth formers already knew our capabilities. There was probably no more than fifteen out of nearly two hundred boys in the sixth form who had any real chance of getting to Oxford or Cambridge. Some in the lower sixth were already being lined up for Oxbridge entrance exams. Cambridge was about forty miles away but Oxford a whole lot more so Cambridge was a nice option for we Chelmsfordians. For me I would have chosen Oxford purely based on the fact that I always supported them in the Boat Race and Cambridge United were arch rivals to Chelmsford City in football's Southern League and, being a staunch City supporter, I really did not like Cambridge one little bit.

The problem was I had no chance of going to either. Some of my mates did have half a chance and some sat the exams and one or two actually got there but in 1966 we were not sure where we would end up when we were eighteen after our A-levels. No doubt in some cases we would be working instead of studying.

But we could dream. Someone, clearly taken with Cambridge, suggested that eight of us had a day out there to suss it out for the future should we ever find ourselves an undergraduate in that fine city. The idea was to split into four groups and hitch hike there during the morning. It would be a race with two different routes selected and a slightly staggered start for the two groups on each route.

Our task was to go to King's College Chapel and sign the visitor's book on arrival with the time inserted. Losers buy the drinks.

We all met at the Public Library in the middle of Chelmsford. I set off with my partner and we had the "via Broomfield route" heading due north. We set up off just ahead of "Stodge" and his partner. The other two groups took the northwest route via Bishop's Stortford.

We soon picked up a lift less than a mile into our route. It was an elderly retired couple out for the day and they were heading out to North Essex and then into Suffolk. We learnt a lesson from them for the future in that the gentleman said that he only picked us up because he knew we were students from a "good school" due to the fact that we had smart long school scarves (actually sixth form scarves on this occasion). If we ever hitched again this would be our essential clothing even in the summer!

The couple were so taken with our "task" that they decided that instead of heading up towards Suffolk they would spend the day in Cambridge instead. So we got our lift all the way there.

The "via Bishop's Stortford" groups had equal success and three of the four groups signed into the visitor's book within twenty minutes of each other just after noon.

Not so, poor old "Stodge" and his partner. They had to walk well over five miles to the other side of the village of Great Waltham before they got picked up. No such luck with just the one lift either; they had to get several. Eventually they arrived at the Chapel at about 3 and no sooner had they signed in they had to turn round and hitch home. This time with the routes reversed for each group.

Another valuable lesson was learnt in the art of hitch hiking apart from the scarves. Our "Good Samaritans" who stopped to give us a lift also said they liked the fact that we were actually walking along and thumbing as opposed to just sitting there waiting for someone to stop. Walking forward and putting your thumb out did become a health and safety issue. One of our number on that day was doing just this in that he heard some cars coming and stuck out his arm, thumb poised. Just as he did so a cyclist was passing. The hand struck the cyclist on the side of the head and nearly knocked him off his bike and into the road. The man desperately struggled to keep his balance and avoid falling into the path of the passing cars. The irony for this cyclist was that he was wearing a crash helmet normally worn by motorcyclists. Our mate's hand hurt like hell as it hit the side of the man's helmet. We all laughed when we heard the story. This particular cyclist was well known to us as we frequently saw him around the town and thought what a silly man he was wearing a crash helmet just to ride a bike when no one else ever did. Given that thousands of people cycled on the roads of Chelmsford every day, we knew of no one ever hurting their heads if they fell off. Elbows? ... Yes, Knees? ...Yes but never a head injury. Cyclist's helmets – that will never catch on we thought! Little did we know!

Back in Cambridge we all set off on our return. To get to Bishop's Stortford we needed the A11 (no motorway in those days) and from Stortford we needed the A414 back to Chelmsford. A lorry soon pulled over. Not one of your large artics of today but a decent size nonetheless. The driver was a very pleasant chap who had not long lived in the country having come over from Jamaica. We fitted in the cab nicely but could not help but notice the sign in front us, which said "Strictly No Passengers", but we said nothing.

Our driver had not the slightest clue of his route he had just been told to follow the A11 from Cambridge then when he saw the sign for the link road across to the A10 he was to take that. It would take him further west into London than the A11 and to a part of the North Circular Road that he was familiar with so he could get back to his depot.

This was sound logic by his bosses but it meant that we would not get to Bishop's Stortford, as our driver would have turned off well before we reached there.

The driver needed something to eat and he stopped at a roadside cafe. He very kindly bought us cheese on toast and it was at this point that we persuaded him that the A11 straight into London would be far quicker for him and still get him to the North Circular and as long as he went west when he arrived at that road he would find his way home.

Steve Little

Trusting us implicitly he agreed. We got to Bishop's Stortford and said goodbye to our newfound friend and sent him on his way. We often wondered whether he did find his way home to his depot before dark or whether he spent the evening driving blindly round the North Circular cursing a couple of know it all schoolboys! We soon picked up another lift and were home in Chelmsford in time for tea. No alarms for the other groups this time but "Stodge" vowed never to do it again.

Therefore, he opted out of the next trip, which was to hitch to the Old Bailey to watch any trial that was on and, for we scholars, to learn something of the judicial processes of our Courts of Law. Again we split into pairs but with "Stodge" staying at home, the pairings were changed. This time I was with Steve Cawley.

The Old Bailey run was out of Chelmsford past the fire station to the A12 and then straight into London, through the City and to the Old Bailey in Holborn, again about forty miles. Steve and I only got as far as the fire station when an elderly gentleman with his grandson in the passenger seat pulled up and offered us a lift to Brentwood, about fifteen miles. Thank you we said and off we went. Once past the Britvic factory we reached the roundabout where we could join the A12. There is a left turn towards Colchester and a right turn towards London at about two o'clock that takes you onto the dual carriageway. Instead of going to his left and round the roundabout the normal way, our driver just turned right and went the wrong way round the roundabout!

Steve looked at me quizzically and frowned. I shrugged. A couple of cars had avoided us but this was not the rush hour and the road was, thankfully, relatively quiet. We had said nothing. It had all happened in the blink of an eye and we were safely on the dual carriageway going the right way. The ten-year-old grandson then said, "Granddad I think you just went the wrong way round that roundabout!"

"Really?" said the old man and he carried on as if nothing had happened.

The Old Bailey was a disappointment we could only get into one trial and we soon found out why there were so many empty seats in the public gallery.

The trial was for attempted GBH using a knife. The offence had taken place in a factory in Sussex and involved four men all of Middle Eastern descent. The accused had drawn a knife on one of the others and the other two had witnessed it.

The problem with this trial was that the four men were from three different countries and once Counsel had asked a question in English it then had to be interpreted for the accused and then in yet another two languages for the other three. The accused's answer was then translated back into English and the other two languages. We stayed an hour and that was enough – only two questions had been asked. One of the keener jurors in a pinstriped suit further held up matters by repeatedly passing notes to the judge who then had to clarify some point.

We left and went off for a coffee and a sandwich ahead of our journey home.

This was the last such hitch hiking escapade through choice. None of our group made it to Cambridge to study but at least we avoided the Old Bailey as well!

19

FROM A SNOWMAN TO A DOLPHIN!

From time to time the school held Sixth Form Dances at the end of the school year. In 1965 it was to be held in early July. I had just turned 16 and completed my O-levels at the end of the fifth year.

The dances were always organised by the senior boys with permission having to be obtained from the Head.

Due to the poor response from the sixth formers an invite was extended to the fifth formers. These dances were not like the Proms the teenagers have today and were low key in comparison.

The summer of '65 had a diversity of music in and around the time of the dance the Number Ones included "Help Me Ronda" by The Beach Boys, "Mr Tambourine Man" by The Byrds, "I Can't Help Myself" by The Four Tops and "Satisfaction" by The Rolling Stones. To come were "I Got You Babe" by Sonny and Cher, "Yesterday" by The Beatles and "Eve of Destruction" by Barry Maguire!

As for the Dance, well it was Ron Snowball and the Snowmen! A local combo of five with the great man Ron on the drums. Their waltzes and foxtrots were top notch apparently. In fact I had experience of their pedigree as my Mum and Dad regularly attended or organised dances and Ron and his men were one of their favourites.

Now that might have been the case if you born in the 1920s but not quite what the teenagers of the 1960s looked for. Something a little "groovier" would be more to our taste but anyway for a 16 year old it was a night out. We were just not quite old enough to pass as 18 and so pubs were more often than not a little beyond us unless we were desperate and went to the real down market spit and sawdust variety like the Royal Steamer in the town, which did not ask any awkward questions!

Typically I was woman less so this at least gave me the chance to size up some options. In our small cul-de-sac of 16 houses there were a number of teenage girls, some older who would not dream of going out with someone younger than them and there were four about my age or a year younger.

I had known these girls since we were toddlers and once they grew up I could never really have the same feeling for them as I remember what they looked like in their nappies!

They were all quite attractive now – there was Susan, Anne, Hilary and Linda. All would probably come to the dance if I asked them, not because they were flattered that I had asked them out but as 15/16 year olds they were probably bored with nothing to do like the rest of us. So which one to dance to the Snowmen, definitely an awkward choice?

I decided on Linda. I knew her parents well as they were friends with my parents. Linda's Mum used to pay the men from the Prudential and United Friendly for us when they collected the fortnightly premiums for various insurances. Linda's family had this ferocious looking Alsatian called "Beauty", a misnomer if ever there was, and because I had to deliver the money and the insurance books personally I had to go through their side gate. As soon as I started to open it "Beauty" would come rushing round from the back garden all snarling and barking – it would bound up to me, skid to a halt and lick me! I was later to find out that the dog was more attracted to me than the daughter of the house was ever likely to be!

Linda's Dad worked with mine at Christy's and they played cricket together. They had a bit of previous in that they had had a falling out about cricket but had recently made up! Her Dad seemed quite pleased that I had asked his Linda to go out with me and would later remark how strange it would be if Linda and me eventually got married! Blimey, that was enough to put anyone off at 16!

So, before all this happened I had to pluck up courage to ask her out. Each day she had to walk past my house on her way to school and for two mornings I stood by the front door to casually walk out and engage her in conversation. Both days she had either left earlier or was not going to school. On the third day there she was. To my surprise she immediately said, "Yes" and we arranged to leave on the Saturday at 7 and walk down to the school.

Flushed with this success I proudly told all my mates at school that day that I had "pulled" and would see them on the Saturday. I saw Linda twice before the Saturday but only gazing at her through Mum's net curtains. Each time she looked more attractive. She was slim with a nice figure, slender legs, decent bosom but her hair was a little bit mousy, still … not bad!

Saturday came and I went and picked her up and was immediately disappointed. I was not expecting her in a ball gown with beautiful bouffant hair and layers of make up but a home knitted cardigan?!

The walk to the school seemed to take longer than my normal brisk mornings walk with Ketley and Bird but we were there in about 30 minutes. She had hardly said anything on the way – quiet rather than rude but already I was beginning to wish I'd asked Susan, Hilary or even Anne!

Despite it being a warm summer evening she never took off her cardigan. We danced the waltz a few times but barely spoke. Ron Snowball churned out his adequate middle of the road stuff that would have delighted our parents and grandparents but most of us there were less motivated and danced out of boredom rather than desire and we longed for a bit of "pop" music.

The evening drew to a close and so did my one date with Linda. We walked home and she was as quiet as before. All the waltzes had been at arm's length and it was the most asexual encounter imaginable. I did slip my arm into hers on the walk back but there was no movement from her. No kiss at the gate. The following week her Dad made his comment about marriage – my only thought was "over my dead body mate"!

...

To all of us the Dance was a big flop the Snowmen had not ignited the audience and had literally melted into the night. Their music was never to be seen in the teenage world again! As for Linda? ... No more dates and much to her Dad's disappointment, perhaps, no wedding bells.

There was no Dance in 1966 as no one wanted another flop on their hands but by the time 1967 came round WE were the potential organisers. Ron Snowball still plied his craft with the middle-aged but he was not for us this time and we sought something that would be a little "way out".

Of course, the Prefect's Room was alive with ideas some so far out that we thought about approaching Procul Harum. They were at Number One with "A Whiter Shade of Pale" and someone knew their lead singer Gary Brooker but we thought they might just be out of our league. We were also looking for something like a heavy rock group.

Biddlecombe and Brunwin took on the organiser mantle. One of them knew a group to provide just what we wanted. We really did need to wipe away the memory of the Snowmen.

The first thing, though, was to get the idea of a different type of dance past the Head, who was probably more Wagner than Snowball and probably thought The Beatles were long haired layabouts. Hughes was Head Boy when the Dance was muted and he somehow managed to hoodwink the Head and we got the go ahead.

Biddlecombe announced that "The Style" would perform at the price we could afford, as tickets were 5 shillings for a single or 8 shillings for a double. So they were booked.

Brunwin was of the opinion that we should organise security at the door to stop undesirables gatecrashing. We had already experienced an unsavoury piece of gatecrashing at a friend's party at his parent's rather large house in the town, quite close to the school, when all the local pubs emptied and turned up at this house. It was like those parties gatecrashed today due to messages sent on the Internet. It took three days to get rid of everyone from our friend's house and just before his parents returned from holiday!

Biddlecombe said he knew of a bouncer at one of the Brentwood Clubs. This man was Ray Dolphin and someone not to be messed with. Such was his reputation that he actually got his name printed on the glossy tickets that Biddlecombe and Brunwin managed to produce for the dance. The ticket read "Ray Dolphin in attendance" at the bottom as if that would deter gatecrashers!

The dance went off without problem although the Head's brief attendance to check on proceedings was short-lived and his frown suggested this was not what he thought was appropriate.

The Style failed to make it in the world of popular music but even now though their name lives on!

20

"GET TREVOR BAILEY OUT OF THE BAR – THE GAME'S FINISHED!"

In July 1966 the Number One in the first week of that July was "Paperback Writer" by the Beatles but "Sunny Afternoon" by the Kinks soon knocked that off top spot.

The football World Cup had started and England had disappointingly drawn the opening game 0-0 with Uruguay and their next game was due at Wembley on Saturday 16th against Mexico.

The KEGS under 18 cricket team for the first and only time had, that summer, entered the Trevor Bailey Shield limited over knock out competition for under 18 teams around Essex. Trevor Bailey was at that time Captain of the Essex County side and had

Days We'll Remember All Our Lives

already had an illustrious career as an England all-rounder. To be eligible for his competition, you had to be Under 18 at the beginning of the summer term so that excluded cricket luminaries at the school like Bennett and Prentice but the KEGS team, led by Paul Biddlecombe had a fair sprinkling of first X1 players with some promising younger Second X1 starlets.

As usual there was little support from the school so Bidders took on the organising role with David "Rowdy" Yates, our cricket master, coerced eventually into supporting us.

Our opening game against the local Chelmsford Club was won with ease against a side brimming with local stars like John Gisby and Ken Hyde who were eventually to get selected for Essex CCC Under 18 Colts.

Perhaps they were over confident but we brushed them aside at a canter.

The next match was against village club Broomfield and it was another comfortable win.

The semi final was scheduled against the Gidea Park Club at the then County Ground at Gidea Park close to the A12 as it by-passed Romford. The date set was Friday 15th July in the early evening. It was imperative it was played as the final was set for the following Monday the 18th July at the (now) County Ground at Chelmsford.

Steve Little

When the KEGS team arrived at the ground by coach provided by the school it was pouring with rain so, to protect their best pitch, Gidea Park moved us to their second pitch where the outfield was not quite as good and the square was fine if not a little soggy.

Bidders won the toss and put the opposition into bat. The cricket ball soon became like a bar of soap and everyone got wet as the persistent drizzle that eventually turned to heavy rain fell throughout. However, the game had to be played out in view of the final on the Monday. Many of the players would have preferred to be at home watching the Hungarians crush the mighty Brazil 3-1 that evening but they had to endure the cold and the rain for the sake of the school and themselves!

The wet outfield restricted a flow of boundaries and Gidea Park managed a meagre 70 or so in 18 overs.

Gurling and I opened the KEGS batting looking like twins as we were similar of stature and both wore our school caps pulled down over our black rimmed unbreakable glasses. The ball was even more slippery than a bar of soap and the poor wicketkeeper had great difficulty in holding onto the ball when missed by the batsmen so we frequently ran byes when he dropped the ball. The partnership grew promisingly.

We both had to wipe our glasses after each ball then, as the bowler ran in, look down at the ground so as to

Days We'll Remember All Our Lives

keep the rain off the lens until the last second when we would then look up and try and play the ball.

With the outfield a morass of puddles it was difficult to get much more than a single run as the ball went nowhere. Gurling was out and a couple of other batsman followed but I was able to help young Ward see the team home. Absolutely soaked to the skin we got back on the coach and went home to watch the football highlights. The scorebook was so wet it fell apart so no full record of the match remains just a fading memory!

The following Monday the weather was as different as could be. The world seemed a better place as goals from Bobby Charlton and Roger Hunt had seen off Mexico and a point against France on the Wednesday would see us progress to the Quarter Finals where we might meet Argentina or West Germany.

The following is a report of our cricket final written for the school magazine by the triumphant captain, Biddlecombe.

"The final was played on the Essex Ground in Chelmsford. Biddlecombe won the toss and "unexpectedly" (as one Southend newspaper put it) put Southend in to bat. They started scoring very quickly, 60 runs in the first ten overs. Catches were not going to hand, and too many extras were being given away. However, the school side tightened its fielding in the second ten overs and Southend could

only manage to score 86 for the loss of 7 wickets in their allotted 20 overs.

Little and Gurling opened but the latter was soon out, caught, trying an adventurous "hook" shot. Little carried his bat for a magnificent unbeaten 54 and the school scored 87 for 6 in only 19 overs.

After the game Trevor Bailey presented the shield bearing his name to Biddlecombe and this trophy is on display in the school. Thanks must be given to our bowlers who performed splendidly.

The school teams can learn several lessons from our success in this competition: that good, quick running between the wickets can win matches and make otherwise low scores look quite respectable; that fast, clean fielding can save runs and get wickets, something not realised by most school teams."

Thus the wise words from a seventeen-year-old captain. When Trevor Bailey, gin and tonic in hand, emerged from the bar to make the presentation he made similar comments about Biddlecombe's team.

What our captain had to say did not reveal all that happened on that evening. The analysis of the match statistics shows that Cronin, our ace bowler, had the highly respectable figures of 2 for 18 in 7 overs including a maiden. This is only half the story. His first over conceded three lots of four byes! The shiny new ball swung in the air so much, plus the inevitable element of nerves, that Cronin bowled the balls a yard or more outside the leg stump. I should know because I was the wicketkeeper and could not lay a hand on any of them!

Another incident that went unreported was when Peter Ward was batting. Now he was a hard hitting and strong lefthander whose strength belied the fact that he was only 15, two years younger than the rest of us.

He hit an over pitched delivery straight into the face of a lad fielding at silly mid off. There was the sickening crunch as the hard ball hit flesh and bone. The unprotected boy collapsed into a heap. Peter Ward ran towards the stricken body and was quickly joined by the rest of us. An official ran onto the field from the pavilion with a first aid kit. Someone shouted that we should get an ambulance, someone else said, no need, as the hospital with its casualty unit was less than a hundred yards away and just over the boundary ropes. The lad stirred.

In all this concern the cricket ball had spiralled off the fielder's head and bounced to the fielder at mid-wicket and he had thrown the ball into the wicketkeeper who had whipped off the bails and shouted "Owzat?" – however, the umpires had ran to help the boy along with the rest of us including Peter who, when the bails were removed, was out of his crease of course.

The boy sat up and laughed, nervously, and we all stepped back in surprise. His forehead had the most perfect round red mark the exact size of a cricket ball perfectly symmetrical in the middle of his forehead and between his hairline and the gap between his eyebrows. The seam of the ball had even left an attractive design and there was a small trace of some of the letters of the ball makers name next to it.

The boy stood up and seemed none the worse from the blow and was even happy to carry on. What luck he had had! Two inches lower and his nose would have been smashed: two inches to the left or right and his eye socket or his temples may not have taken the blow quite so well.

The Southend captain enquired of the umpires whether Peter was in or out. The umpires met in the middle of the wicket to discuss their decision and declared it was a "dead ball" (very nearly a dead fielder!) and Peter was able to carry on with his innings and the fielder with his newly acquired "tattoo" was moved to the third man boundary.

21

WHO WOULD LIKE TO BUY THESE TICK ……? DAMN!

By the Spring of 1967 we are all either seventeen or eighteen. As teenagers we had seen the arrival of the Beatles and all similar pop groups, as they were then called, like the Kinks, Hollies, Rolling Stones, Animals and so on. Tamla Motown came over from Detroit and took us by storm. Our music tastes moved away from the more conventional sounds of some groups and artistes. As the Beatles became more "way out" so did we.

A new type of music stirred up we sophisticates. Soul and R&B became our mantra, as well as a liking for the "old" stuff at our discos in run down church halls where we had the opportunity to pick up "birds", we now had Otis Redding as our stand out hero.

This was not the Otis Redding that people only seem to remember today. If you mention his name now

they say "Oh he did "Sittin' on the Dock of the Bay""
– we have to tell them that was about as un-Otis as it was possible to get. Firstly it was released after his death and secondly it was like comparing "Twist and Shout" with "Yesterday".

In today's terminology of the teenager it would be "cool" to say you liked this music with its Afro-Caribbean roots. There had been an influx of West Indians, in particular, to the UK in the fifties and early sixties and this was to influence our choice of music in this country. The BBC still had the Light Programme and the Home Service, which were very Radio 3 and 4. Of course, Radios 1 to 4 had not yet been invented but in southern England we had pirate radio ships moored off the Essex coast and in the Thames Estuary, with Radio Luxemburg still also available, and they introduced us to these American Soul and R&B singers.

Such was the success of the groups and artistes that many of them came over here to put on a series of concerts. The self appointed "cool" dude in the Prefect's Room was Brunwin, destined to be Head Boy in the 1967-1968 school year and currently in that Spring a boarder at the school.

He had seen a concert advertised at the Hammersmith Empire that included Booker T and the MGs, Sam & Dave, Arthur Conley, Carla Thomas and the great man, Otis, himself.

Brunwin sought out support and we fell over ourselves rushing to order tickets from him. The Empire is some 50 miles from Chelmsford and how were 20 or so of us to get there? Brunwin had this point covered. We'll go during the week in the school term and get a coach through the school and perhaps the Head will pay for it. Being a boarder Brunwin saw the Head more than we did and had his ear.

Fine said the Head a good cultural evening! Brunwin had sold him on the idea that we were going to a concert and that was sort of true but the Head had not heard of this "classical singer" Redding but wished us an enjoyable evening nonetheless!

Brunwin then ran into his first setback. To have a school trip we needed to take a master with us and the Head was sure any one of his staff would like an evening of sophisticated music! Brunwin knew that any of the masters would look more into what the content of the concert was and would not want to accompany us when they found out. This, indeed, proved to be the case.

For the first time in his life Brunwin was stumped for an answer. Then someone made a valuable suggestion. Mr Grant, History, was a fellow from an Oxford or Cambridge college and to help out this old college Mr Grant had agreed to take on a young graduate who was now studying for his Masters degree in History. This young man was only about four years older than us and was more Mozart than Otis. He was a decent chap and with a lot of cajoling from Brunwin agreed to accompany us on the coach and attend the concert – we paid for his ticket.

The coach was booked for a Tuesday night and we spent all day longing for the bell at the end of the day when we could all get into our flares and brightly coloured shirts and head off to West London to see the great man.

The journey would take about two and a half hours through the rush hour traffic to Hammersmith and we were due to leave at 4.30. During the day Brunwin had received some bad news. Two lads who had bought tickets dropped out. It was too late to get replacements so Brunwin came up with the idea that he would sell the tickets outside the Empire. We could make a decent amount of money on it as the concert was a sell out and the demand would be immense and ticket touts were prevalent in those days outside theatres and sports grounds even more than today. So whilst he might have competition Brunwin was looking forward to getting a handsome profit!

The coach pulled up right outside the entrance to the Empire. Our Oxbridge man took a low profile as we reached the pavement the last thing he wanted was to be seen in charge of a crocodile of teenagers clearly on a school trip!

However, we looked somewhat out of place standing there, as we seemed to be the only white faces amongst the happy throng of black people. Although we had a smattering of West Indians living in Chelmsford most of us had never seen so many in one place before.

Brunwin could not believe his luck when he saw so many and knew that the demand for his two spare tickets would be so great he could really make a killing and we could put the profit towards the Prefect's Room kitty to be spent on something important at a later date.

He told us he would go to the steps to the theatre to make his pitch and take on the mantle of the famous tout of that time, Stan Flashman. He still had the tickets in his pocket. He went up three steps and pulled the tickets from his back pocket. "Who would like to buy these tick…...?" That was as far as he got a black hand whipped them from his grasp and the culprit disappeared back into the throng.

Tail between his legs Brunwin came back to us. Instead of profit for our funds that kitty would now have to buy the tickets. Never mind it was a good idea at the time!

We had been used to the Odeon in Chelmsford as our largest local cinema/theatre but the Hammersmith Empire was something else. We had good seats up in the circle and when the safety curtain opened and revealed the stage we realised just how far away we were.

As we expected, there were not many white faces in the audience. The music started up and on came the compere, Emperor Rosko, then a pirate DJ and later to join Radio 1. He told us that tonight's performance was being taped and would form part of the LP to be released after the tour had finished. Booker T came on and with his MGs did his classic "Green Onions".

It was usual in those days for audiences to sit and listen and politely applaud. Not here though. Everyone (well apart from our Oxbridge man) was up dancing to the music. The roof nearly came off when the great man came on with his epic "Can't Turn You Loose" and even the Oxbridge man was out of his seat but perhaps that was just so he could see!

Brunwin soon got over his disappointment of not exploiting the ticket black market and we all congratulated him on his foresight in booking us in to see Otis, poignantly this was one of the last times Otis performed because by the Autumn he was dead – killed in a plane crash. He had just recorded "Sittin' on the Dock of the Bay" when he died but had run out of recording studio time when he had to leave for a flight. In the last "take" he forgot the words and so whistled through the last part. He was due to return to the studio when he was next in LA to finish it off. He died before this could happen and the recording company left the song as it was - hence the whistling!

We know what happened to Otis but what of our Oxbridge man without whom we could never have had such a wonderful experience and we still wonder if he remembers us?

(This piece is dedicated to the memory of Ben Brunwin, someone who was full of life and a really good bloke who so tragically died of leukaemia in 2008)

22

IT'S MY PARTY AND I'M DEFINITELY GOING TO HAVE MARILYN MONROE!

During the winter of the Shenfield party and into the following summer I hosted two parties at my parents' house. The first was with my parents there with my cousin Hazel (no longer suffering with her blood pressure) and her husband, Brian, keeping them company. They were in the living room with the TV and we were in the "Lounge" as we would call it today but in those days it was called the "Front Room" but in our case it was actually a room in the back of the house!

There was the usual excess of boys. Through a current liaison of one of our number, eight girls, who were all from the High School, were persuaded to come along. This was the usual set up where the girls would all "get off" with one of us in turn but with the inevitable result that some of us would remain womanless and our barren spell from scoring would continue for another week. The girls were all very pleasant and we boys circled like strutting peacocks in the mating season but with less bravado when push came to shove. It was the brash, more confident ones that picked up the girls and the rest would inevitably end up sitting around the outside of the room bemoaning our luck. This would all happen a little later in the evening on this occasion. We were a little young for the "lights out straight away" smooch and the girls suggested that we play games. So off two of them went to find my Mum. They came back with a curtain ring and a large ball of wool and an orange.

The first game was "pass the ring". This we had to do along a length of wool that was attached to each of the two teams. The novelty of the game and a definite icebreaker was that the length of wool went down the inside of the shirt or blouse front of one person and up the leg of the trousers or skirt of the next. The ring was then passed along and the first team to get it from one end to the other were the winners. Well, great hilarity especially when the girls had to pass the wool UP their skirts and with a little pull the front of their skirts would rise up and they would have great difficulty maintaining their modesty!

Once this was over we then played the "Pass the Orange under the Chin" game and this meant we got close up and personal to a girl or two but sometimes to another bloke in view of the boys outnumbering the girls.

There was no alcohol but some good music playing on my Dad's brilliant gramophone that gave a much better sound than the usual Dansette player. After the hilarious games the slow records came on and seven boys got dancing with seven of the girls, which on this occasion left one girl and five boys. Unfortunately this girl, who we knew would be a very pleasant young lady was, let's say, a size 16 whereas the other girls were 8s or 10s. Most of us knew the girl's brother and this made things difficult because she apparently got upset that she was left on the shelf, as it were, but to "get off with her" carried a bit of a stigma, boys being what they are. Anyway the rest of the couples were smooching away and getting to know each other better. For once being the host I thought I might have the first choice but the more likely lads were straight in and I was left dancing with Judith. She was attractive without being pretty and seemed good fun - well at least she laughed at my attempt at wit. I always thought this to be a good sign!

The favourite party music at that time would be slow ones like "You've Lost That Loving Feeling" by the Righteous Brothers and, in particular, an EP by a singer-songwriter called Arthur Alexander. The EP had two tracks on each side of a vinyl 45-rpm record and this meant that you had a longer clinch with the girl as the record did not have to be changed quite so quickly. So with dimmed lights the proceedings got more intense with an audience of the five lads and the girl. The six of them had nowhere to go apart from to their own homes. It was invariably the case that the friend you were travelling home with was one of those with a partner so there was no option but to sit and wait until the friend decided to leave or the party came to an end.

I fancied going out with Judith and we did eventually manage one date and we got on well. The problem was firstly she was not, unlike me, on the telephone. Secondly, she lived so far out in the sticks that her last evening bus was about 7pm. We could have met after school but the Girls High School just up the road from KEGS came out earlier than us (we always assumed this was deliberate so as to avoid contact) and Judith had to get her one bus at about 3.45 and we boys did not come out of school until just after that. So there it was, a match maybe made in heaven but it was just impractical to meet but I'd see her once more when we bumped into each other when I was playing football against her village side and she was watching. I wonder where she is now?

It is an odd fact that I met and eventually was to marry a girl with almost the same character, looks and ability to laugh at my jokes. She also lived in the back of beyond and had no telephone and the same bus problem BUT the one difference was that I passed by driving test two weeks after meeting her and at least I was able to give her a lift home if I borrowed my Dad's car!

Steve Little

Getting back to the bunch of girls. Seven of us got off all right although as I've said any relationship with Judith was not going to be anything that would go any further but the others carried on with their girls and there followed a series of social events that the girls came to when the relationships continued although there were some swaps along the way. At future parties we had to agree that the size 16 girl had to be accommodated and in the end someone took the plunge and found what a lovely person she was!

Some of the girls were invited to a second party at my house within the year. This time there were no parents and we were allowed some alcohol. Attendance was strictly by invitation and to be controlled. There had been a few other social gatherings with the group of girls and a new girl had joined their number. She was gorgeous. She had blond hair and was, for 16 years of age, a voluptuous Marilyn Monroe look alike.

The boys would always look forward to any party and discuss the spare talent likely to be on view before hand. "Marilyn" was the only talk of our group and we all had our eyes firmly set on getting off with her. I was determined that as host I was to have first crack at "Marilyn" when the first record (all slow ones and with the lights low from the start) was put on.

The usual ones were there Hughes, Gunn, Stoneham, Ottley, Lemon, Green, Mason, Haworth and a few others. Some had their girls there already and some were on the hunt that evening.

First dance and I am introducing the record and giving the go ahead and I'm up on my feet way ahead of the rest of the blokes and straight in with a dance with "Marilyn" with a polite "Would you like to Dance?" She accepted without, it has to be said, a lot of gusto and my first mistake was to offer my left hand to hold hers like you would for a waltz. Big mistake! Not at all romantic and she clasped my hand and the look in her eye told me immediately that she would only be having this one dance with this dud!

True enough Arthur Alexander had not even got to the second track on the EP when she said "Thank you" and sat down and Phil Mason jumped in, pulled her to her feet and clasped her in the more traditional hug dance rather than my formal waltz position.

So, I was cast into the wilderness. Everyone else was fixed up except me and the three others who were destined to watch from the dark corners of the room. Even size 16 was swept off her feet and thus the host had, yet again, ended up a wallflower.

"Marilyn" and Phil Mason seemed to be getting on well and claimed an armchair with "Marilyn" on Phil's lap - the lucky beggar! What happened next only fully emerged the next morning when there was the traditional inquest about the night before as some of the blokes came round and helped clear up.

Apparently whilst having a snog Phil's hand was resting on "Marilyn's" thigh on top of her short skirt and squeezing as and when required to stimulate the simmering relationship. One of the lads, who to protect his reputation will remain anonymous, idly rubbed the beauty's thigh INSIDE her skirt and met Phil's hand as he moved up!

Within minutes "Marilyn" and our friend had left the room and gone into the living room and locked the door. It was the room that led to the kitchen where the drink was. I was watchful about any larking about especially as Mum and Dad forbade me for example to allow anyone upstairs unless it was for the toilet and I was now not in control.

Ten minutes went by and the couple were still locked in. Then twenty and then half an hour by which time we were getting thirsty and I was getting annoyed. The back door had also been locked and the curtains drawn so there was no way I had of seeing what they were doing or getting them out of there.

Eventually they came out and left without so much as a by your leave! At school on Monday I closely questioned our friend as to why he was in there so long. The only thing he would say was that it took an age to get her bra catch undone! Now I should say relationships were not as casual and "full on" from the start, as it were, as they are in the modern day but only he and she knows what went on.

I kept all this from Mum and Dad but I never saw "Marilyn" again as the relationship soon folded with her man.

23

I REALLY WOULD LIKE TO LOOK LIKE ROGER MOORE

Image was so important to we teenagers at this time when fashion and trends were changing by the week and at times it was difficult to keep up.

We largely missed the era of the Elvis greased up quiff but got caught up in the Beatles long hair, then the Rolling Stones with even longer hair then came the flower power California dreaming era when we all wanted to be like Scott Walker or George Harrison in his Hari Krishna phase.

In between that we had the David Frost look, which was hair combed forward and turned up at the front and was the look he wore on That Was The Week That Was – I recall I took on that style at the age of fourteen. One Saturday night when the whole family had met up at my Nan's for tea my straight laced military minded Uncle Ken asked me what on earth I had done to my hair – I said it was the "Frost look" to which he said, with much guffawing from the whole family, that my hair looked more like it had caught the frost! Sunday morning it reverted to the 14-year-old plain mop!

Roger Moore was appearing in The Saint series based on the Leslie Charteris hero. Mr Moore had the most brilliant slicked up and combed back style, which many of us thought was better than what Elvis had and Roger, after all, was British!

Our mate, Mike Mottram, lived just round the corner from me, next to the Ketley's and also went to the school. He was from a fairly staid Catholic family background. He had an attractive older sister but too old for the likes of us to be that interested in. Mike had a mop just like me but then one Monday morning he turned up at school with a "Roger Moore" – all slicked back with brylcream and with a "boston" across the back of this wonderful hairstyle. For the next five years he looked exactly the same every day as if it was a wig with never a hair out of place. For all we know he might have kept the style right through his life just like Roger Moore including, perhaps, a little help from "Just for Men".

Image was important but families had little money to buy designer type clothes like parents do for teenagers today mainly because our parents had no money or perhaps it was just the case that they had more sense!

Steve Little

My Mum's biggest concern for me was teenage spots or more seriously acne. In her teenage years boys suffered from acne due to the poor diets of the 30s. In the 50s and 60s diets were better but there was a bit of acne about. She inspected me every week for teenage spots and would love to pinch the blackheads from my 13-year-old face. This got me into a regular spell in front of her mirror looking for the start of a spot. When we look back there were few boys in the school who had a serious spot problem like we sometimes see today. Perhaps their Mums were also on weekly spot watch like mine or perhaps we were fit and ate well with the right foods and washed well. My biggest bugbear as a teenager was chilblains, which are almost unheard of today, but every winter we got them so it must have been something in our diets – probably suet puddings that were awful! Boils were a fading problem by the sixties but a large, one-off, uncomfortable boil-like spot appeared every now and then.

I was paranoid about spot picking in front of the mirror and don't suppose I was alone in this. I once had a spot on an appendage shielded from view and was relieved that it was just an enormous blackhead, which I gleefully pinched and was so proud of the minor "operation" that I had to share the news with my friends, who looked at me as if I truly was mad! So obsessed did I become about blackheads that I spent two weeks trying to pinch these two black blemishes right below my eyes until it suddenly dawned on me that that they were my tear ducts – how sad was that?!

As we got beyond the mid-sixties, the hairstyles were more outrageous and beards came to the fore along with flower power and the British groups that copied the west coast of America look (think Roy Wood of Wizzard and you'll know what I mean!). We sixth formers in 1966 to 1968 not only felt that the school would clamp down on long hair but for us to grow a beard of any substance would probably take the whole school year to do so and then would look like a moth eaten, wispy lot of bum fluff as our Mums and Dads used to call it. Some sixth formers were still only shaving twice a week such was the lack of effective stubble growth. In fact, it was somewhat embarrassing in that some girls we came across had a better mini moustache than we could ever hope for!

With rules on school uniform strictly enforced, our boys always looked smart and it was a little bit of an urban myth that teenagers were all hair and kaftans but of course there was no money and we could not afford such things.

Now some boys, once in the sixth form, could get reasonably well paid summer jobs and would allow them to have money to perhaps buy one of two Carnaby Street type items to get one up on the rest of us.

Terry Ketley was the first of our group of friends to earn some good money.

He worked for the Parks Department during the summer holidays and spent most days mowing the Council Parks and the grass around the many Council Estates in Chelmsford. It was quite well paid. Hipsters came into vogue and Terry used his hard earned money to buy a pair. Even Terry would agree that he had not been the most sartorially orientated person having been brought up in a typical, loving ordinary home where traditional, functional clothes and not many of them were the norm.

Anyway he bought these hipsters. The design was such that, unlike most trousers, they fitted low round your hips and not your waist. In the 60s they had wide belts and were tight round the bottom area and thighs with a bit of a flare in the leg.

Now up until he was about 15 Terry was a big lad but when he started looking to go out with girls he suddenly lost some weight and got extremely lithe and slim. There was no point wearing hipsters if you carried weight because you looked all arse and pockets.

So Terry now fitted into these hipsters and looked fine. The problem was that the trousers he had were the most outrageously designed check monstrosity that you could possibly imagine. He defended the choice in that the girls could not miss him and he would stand out at the parties and discos he was likely to attend. We just laughed but he maintains to this day that the hipsters worked!

Eventually we all followed his lead but chose something a little more subtle in fact my Mum was able to get me a pair of hipster grey trousers to wear for school, grey and black being the only colours we were allowed to wear. They did not compete at all with Terry's and had no effect on the girls whatsoever!

Dress sense remained very ordinary and jeans were considered something you played football in over the park and were not the designer wear of today. Ties were still worn for many outings by our fathers and we wore them the whole way through school. If you get a chance look at an old film of the 1966 World Cup Final, look at how many of the crowd, mainly men, are wearing jackets and ties!

Many girls, including my wife to be, made their own dresses for discos and parties etc. - something very rare today.

Well apart from the Mottram/Moore slick look and my very short-lived Frost look, other styles were thin on the ground. Most of us tried to cope with the unruly mop. Brylcream was not favoured by most as we all wanted to be "Mods" whereas slicked hair made us look more like "Rockers" and Mottram had already cornered the Roger Moore look and we could not be seen to be copying someone else's idea. So in the sixties the normal look for us was non-brylcream, longish to the top of the ears with perhaps a "boston" across the back just above the neck. It was where the bottom of the hair was cut in a straight line.

Some of my friends had great hair. Ian Robinson, who became Brown when his Mum remarried, had the most brilliant brown, curled hair. If only mine looked like that I thought at the time and I'd have given anything for it. So it was a very nasty surprise when I bumped into Ian over ten years after we had left the school and he had no hair on top at all!

Simon Hughes had a kiss curl on his blond locks and that just about survives to this day. Steve Cawley has the same hair today as when he was 4! There is the odd fleck of grey though.

The rest of us are in varying stages of greyness and lack of. Nigel Ottley is a curious case. I had known him from when we were seven. I had not seen him for over 30 years after we left KEGS but when we made contact in the late 90s by telephone one of the first things he said to me was that whilst he looked like he was losing his hair when he was eleven, due to his high forehead, it had not got any worse! It was true!

Funny looking back how we all craved to look so attractive to the opposite sex but some had the ability to pick up girls as easy as wink. Ordinary mortals like me just struggled!

24

"AFTER THIS NEXT RECORD WE'LL ASK THE NEAREST GIRL TO US TO DANCE!"

The winter of 1966/1967 had been a little bit barren on the girlfriend front. I had met Linda M at a dance in the late summer of 1966 and we had been out to the pictures a couple of times and got on well. The trouble was she was not on the telephone and I had to rely on her to contact me for a date. Not an ideal scenario.

I liked her a lot – she was petite and attractive. She had a friend that "Stodge" went out with after he met her at the same dance as I met Linda. I remember going out with Linda the evening after the Aberfan disaster where so many people particularly children in the school there were killed. It was a bit of a sombre evening.

After a couple of weeks she did not bother to call and that was that. Years later I heard that she had prospered well and married a chap from her school.

So over Christmas and New Year it was drinking that kept us going with no girlfriends. "Stodge's" relationship with Linda's friend had also foundered and we were back on the shelf. I was now playing football for Westlea United in a higher division of the Mid Essex League than I had with Christy's Sports. I always got a game as my Dad was manager but at the end of January I strained my hamstring and was out of action.

Most of my friends would be 18 during this school year and we all hoped there would be a few parties or evenings drinking down the pub to celebrate. The problem was we had no money. The pay from the 1966 summer jobs had gone and the cash from pay from the Post Office where we had been the Christmas relief postmen had been spent on Christmas presents and the Christmas Eve and New Year's Eve drink ups.

So as we began to reach this age milestone when we could legally buy a drink in a pub (!) we hoped there would be a party or something where we had some chance of picking up a girl for some romance.

Not many parents were prepared to give up their houses to allow a party but Dick Green's were and at the end of February 1967 we were to celebrate his 18th. Most of our group of eight or so that went round together would not celebrate their birthdays until the Spring or Summer. So we all got our invites to the Green residence in Danbury a few miles outside of Chelmsford for February 25th. The invite did have a sting in its tail for "Stodge" and me and that was that to go we had to take a girl. As puzzling as this might seem, the reason given was that we were less likely to get drunk if we were with a girl because we would, literally in some cases, have more to handle than a pint!

By now we were into February. "Stodge" and me could at least save our money on buying Valentine's cards, as it was now a forlorn hope that we might have someone to send one to. We desperately did not wish to miss out on Green's party as most of our friends were seeing a girl and would be allowed to go.

We tried to persuade Green to change his mind but his Mum was adamant that she did not want any of us being sick on her lovely carpets or in her rose beds! What chance did we now have of going?

Suddenly there was lifeline! One of the girls at the Tech High School had booked a hall in the Moulsham area just south of the town and was to hold a Valentine's Disco. The response from the boys at her school had been poor but she had a lot of girls coming. Desperate to even up the numbers she contacted the Grammar School through one of the Prefects. The dance was on the Saturday night, the 11th. We did not know about this until the Thursday before and much changing of plans went on amongst some of us, not me though as I was doing nothing anyway, to ensure we could go.

So we turned up. Quite a few of us were single and we spent the first part of the evening standing around eying up the girls in the time honoured tradition but really trying to pluck up courage to ask one to dance. On reflection it was not the asking that was the problem but the awful rejection and humiliation if the girl said no. With "Stodge" and me being out of practice, as it were, we missed all the "bombshell" girls as the suave professional "picker uppers" like Hughes and Gunn had creamed off the best talent.

Despite being short of boys at one point the week before our hostess now had too many boys and the old familiar tale of us standing round bemoaning our luck and saying how crap the evening was, even when, like this, it wasn't really!

The Disco was extremely noisy. The Number One that week was "I'm a Believer" by the Monkees from their current hit TV series – so decent to dance to but this was sandwiched between the Numbers Ones from early 1967 of "Green Green Grass of Home" by Tom Jones, "Release Me" by Englebert Humperdink and "Something Stupid" by Frank and Nancy Sinatra. Hardly "rave" music but OK perhaps for a smooch. The DJ did find some loud stuff however and in the small hall it eventually became so loud you could hardly speak to one another.

At about nine there was a break so a group of "girl-less" blokes went down the nearest Pub. There were about six of us. Ben Brunwin, Head Boy in waiting, bought us all a pint. This was a magnanimous gesture as the rest of us would never have bought such a large round in view of cost and would only buy in twos or threes! Ben, whose Mum was Boarding House Matron and lived there with her son and daughter, always seemed to have cash. When he went out with a certain young lady in the next school year their date would consist of a two-hour taxi drive round Chelmsford just to have a chat and "be different" – must have cost him a fortune!

Anyway, with "Stodge", I walked back from the Pub and we bemoaned our luck. This was really just an excuse for our lack of ability in picking up or chatting up girls. Of course, we had not done much to help ourselves perhaps waiting for a girl to make the first move – unfortunately those days were some way off!

Perhaps fortified by our pint of Tartan Bitter we decided to be more positive when we got back to the hall. The Disco had started up again just as noisily as before. Our positive move was to stand in the middle of the rather small dance floor instead of round the side, as if that would make any difference! A few couples were now sitting out exchanging kisses and addresses.

"Bloody hell!" said "Stodge" looking at his watch, "it's nearly ten and it finishes at half past, if we're going to get to Green's party we'd better do something. If we fail tonight it will only leave us next week."

"Right," I shouted back, "after this next record we'll ask the nearest girl to us to dance!"

"What did you say?" he shouted back above Davy Jones on lead vocal with the Monkees.

"I said," shouting even louder, "after this next record we'll ask the nearest girl to us to dance!"

Davy got to the end of the song and there was a very brief lull. I spun one way and "Stodge" went the other. There was this female back with dark brown hair down to her neck. She was wearing an extremely flowery and, as it turned out, homemade frock. For a moment and just before she turned round in response to my tap on her back, I just hoped and prayed that she was not wearing glasses, had a big nose or goofy teeth or perhaps all three!

I need not have worried and she was even quite attractive! I was not warmed up at all having not had a dance all evening and had just come in from the cold night air. She on the other hand had been dancing all night and, as she was later to admit, was a bit sweaty.

The usual ritual followed of trying to confirm our names above the din and I found out she was Chris. We were still shouting at each other when the song came to an end and suddenly had to talk softly. However, before we could exchange further pleasantries the DJ was out on the floor with his mike. "Now everyone, we have less than half an hour to go and all you couples want a few smoochie ones to get closer so here we go with Englebert Humperdink's latest, a nice slow one."

Of course, he wanted us all to get close and cuddly and he wanted to create an atmosphere of "Love" – however, he missed the irony in that the first two lines of Englebert's song are, "Please release me let me go, for I don't love you anymore".

The DJ went on, "Now as it's Valentine's I want you all to kiss right through the record – that'll help you all!"

I looked at Chris a bit sheepishly. We'd had one dance and now we were to kiss full throttle for about three minutes non-stop. Well, we lasted about two and decided to sit down. There being a dearth of chairs I sat down and she sat on my lap. With the old hamstring still a bit tight and Chris being a nicely rounded size 12 I had to manoeuvre to ensure my chances of playing football the next week would not be set back by another injury to the same thigh.

The quieter music meant we could talk a bit more. I cracked a lame joke and she laughed, that was a good sign I thought, as usually the girls are embarrassed for me at my attempt at humour!

Ten minutes went by and we had another kiss or two. Then her friend came over and said to her that if she wanted a lift home they were leaving after the next song.

The DJ decided that his closing numbers would be noisy bopping ones so Chris and I got up to dance. It soon came to an end and she got her coat and as she was leaving the next loud song started. I asked if she would like to go out next week. She said, "Yes" and I asked if she was on the phone or not. She said not; so fearing a Linda or Judith scenario I asked Chris for her address and said I would write with details of next week and she would have my address and phone number. She said fine and, shouting, gave me her address that I desperately tried to memorise.

She went off into the night and I wondered if I would ever see her again.

She did phone me on the Wednesday evening as I requested in my letter, we did go out that next Saturday to see, bizarrely, "Drop Dead Darling" at the pictures! The following week we went to Green's party and no one was sick on Mrs Green's carpets or her roses and me and Chris? -Still together more than 40 years on!

25

"YOU KNOW WHAT? – THIS IS A MENTAL HOME!"

For some of us Geography was one of our favourite subjects mainly because it was interesting for the most part whether it was Physical Geography, Geology, Climatology or whatever.

We had good teachers throughout the time we spent at KEGS with Ken "Noggs" Newman to the fore who told us that if we wrote down what he told us and learnt it we would pass our O-level or even A-level with ease. We were not so sure about the "with ease" but we all did fine.

We also had Field Trips to enjoy, which were not only, as it turned out, ways of helping with the subject but also as part of our development as teenage young men!

Steve Little

For the first trip we were a little too young to sample the delights of the pubs in Swanage but did try and were successful at getting a drink in one, yet the whole time we sat there drinking our half pints we were looking over our shoulders for the Law to turn up!

We did learn a lot from Ken Newman and Michael "Mumbles" Turner on the many geographical phenomena of the region particularly the Isle of Purbeck, Lulworth Cove, Chesil Beach and so on.

There was a local river that had three names, Piddle, Puddle or Trent that made us smile and giggle.

We found fossils embedded in rocks along the beaches – fascinating!

We visited small villages with funny names like Worth Matravers.

One problem we had was the weather. It rained most days and I can remember a damp walk along Hurst Castle spit (another phenomenon of geographical interest apparently) but it was disappointing to get to the end of it and find Hurst Castle a very unattractive edifice looking more like a Second World War defence construction.

On the way back our morale was low as the gale force wind picked up and the rain lashed down. However, Nige "Otter" Ottley led community singing to lift our spirits so there we were a bedraggled rabble belting out such classics as "House of the Rising Sun".

"Otter" was to have a greater claim to fame when we spent another subsequent field trip in North Wales at Barmouth.

...

By the time we went to Barmouth we were nearly two years older than the Swanage trip and now we were well into pub drinking and girls and all considered ourselves to be God's gift to the Swinging Sixties!

The tedious cross-country journey from Chelmsford by coach took most of the first day. Very few motorways or fast roads existed and it was a slow drive up the A5 and into Wales.

Barmouth, for those who do not know, was and remains an area of fascinating geographical interest particularly as it was affected by glaciation during the Ice Age. Quite frankly we were more interested in what the pubs were like and whether the local girls were up to much!

Ken Newman, as well prepared as usual, taught us a lot about the area. We went up to Cader Idris, Snowdon, the falls at Betws-y-Coed and all the other geomorphologic places of interest.

We also liked the pubs and thoroughly enjoyed our few days in Barmouth and contributed greatly to the finances of the town, particularly the local brewery. One unusual drinking spot was the little station across the bridge spanning the estuary from

Barmouth, which is at the end of the railway line. You could walk across the bridge but there was no road. A small platform with a waiting room was at the other side. One day we had to walk from the town across to the other side using the bridge. The rain and wind, just like we had experienced when on Hurst Castle spit, blew straight down the estuary towards the sea. It was bitterly cold although it was early spring. When we got across the bridge our left sides were soaked but our right sides, protected from the wind and rain, were completely dry.

We looked an unusual sight, as we went into the waiting room to dry off before proceeding further. Lo and behold we could not believe it but there was a bar there! So at eleven in the morning we clubbed together our meagre resources and just about had enough to buy a half pint of Watney's Red Barrel each – it was the first and only time I enjoyed it!

To our dismay the talent in the town was disappointing although we did chat up a couple of counter girls in Woolworth's who were very Welsh. They asked us where we came from and we said Chelmsford. They then asked where that was and when we said Essex one of the girls asked if we might have run into her boyfriend who was serving in the Army at Aldershot! We showed her a map book on sale on her counter and where Aldershot was in relation to Chelmsford. Her response was – not far then!

On another day we had an exercise on map reading and were split into groups and we had to find a route from one place on a map back to the hotel by plotting our way using map references – a bit like a walking treasure hunt!

Some of the lads were good map-readers and some were not. "Otter" thought he was very good at it and confidently led his group on a footpath into some very beautiful gardens of a large house along what he erroneously thought was a public footpath when, in fact, it was to prove to be a very private place.

Needing confirmation that the group were on the right track, "Otter" walked over to a man sitting on a bench who was gazing across the manicured lawns. Map in hand "Otter" stood above the man and said, "Excuse me, are we on the right path to Barmouth?" The man looked up but said nothing. Bearing in mind there were quite a few locals who only seemed to speak Welsh (well, at least when we English were around!) "Otter" repeated his request.

The man took the map and looked at it. He turned it up the other way and then turned it over and studied the back of the page on which there was nothing. At which point he folded the map into as small a shape as he could, stuffed it into his jacket pocket, stood up and walked off.

"Otter" stood there bemused. The rest of the group stood about thirty yards away even more bemused by what was going on.

"Hang on a minute," said "Otter", "Excuse me," he said walking after the man who continued to ignore him, "Excuse me."

At this point two men in white coats came from behind a hedge and grabbed the man by the arms and led him off towards the house speaking to "Otter" over their shoulders. "Otter" politely asked for his map back and then came back towards the group looking a little flushed.

"Sorry chaps, just checked the map again, this is a mental hospital and we need to go that way," he said pointing in the direction they had just come from. They all turned and followed him, not another word was said about the incident.

During our stay, we did have three evenings when we could enjoy the pubs and as usual on the last night several over imbibed none more so than Ian Brown. On the way back to the hotel Ian was, like some of the rest of us, desperate to relieve himself after consuming a large number of pints. The tide was right in up to the sea wall and he stood on the parapet and decided to wee into the sea. Some others joined in. Shouting with joy and exhilaration of doing something "different" they did not allow for the onshore gusts of winds and ended up with most of their wee going down the front of their trousers!

Ken Newman was not amused when we very noisily got back to the hotel and we managed to whisk Brown past him disguising Ian's drunken condition.

For that night we nicknamed him "Incapability Brown"!

The next day we were off home after breakfast and had a coach trip of several hours to endure. Not something that is normally that enjoyable if you are feeling more than a little liverish.

"Incapability" was a revelation with no apparent after effects from the night before as he tucked into a full Welsh!

Not too many miles along the route he deposited the full Welsh along the side of the A5!

Ken Newman to this day remembers the incident and also recalls about the only time he lost his cool as a teacher. This was over an incident that had happened back at the hotel. We were having breakfast when there was a commotion in the room immediately above us. Apparently the two boys sharing the room were playing an impromptu football match using a piece of newspaper rolled up into a ball.

The problem was that such was the clomping of feet the ceiling in the dining room shook and pieces of it dropped into our porridge and bacon and egg. Ken flew upstairs and admonished the boys – it was the only time we ever saw him annoyed.

As for these trips helping us with our studies, well they did!

Ironically when we sat our exams set by the Oxford and Cambridge Examining Board the map area chosen on which we had to answer questions on geomorphologic points and plot cross sections along contour lines etc. was of … … The Estuary at Barmouth! We all wished we had listened a bit more of what Ken Newman told us on the trip rather than concerning ourselves more on where we were drinking that evening!

26

THE IMPORTANCE OF BEING THE HEAD BOY

The 1966–1967 school year saw Simon Hughes as our Head Boy. He has had to endure the same question many times in recent years answering that "No" he is not the Simon Hughes from the LibDems nor Simon Hughes the ex-cricketer and now cricket writer on the Daily Telegraph and TV presenter. To me he is the Simon Hughes who I had known since I was seven. He did go on to do rather well after leaving the school but did not become quite so well known as his namesakes!

Duties of a Head Boy are varied in a large school but there are certain perks and responsibilities that come your way.

For Simon one such was a visit with the Head to another school in the county to meet, among others, Sir Stanley Rous who was then the President of FIFA, football's worldwide governing body. The meeting was very brief. The guests all lined up and there was a mere handshake with the great man and he asked what school the person came from and then moved on. The amusing thing about the day was that there were hordes of American children there and they all thought they were about to meet royalty and as Sir Stanley was a slightly balding middle-aged man they thought at first he was Prince Philip. Their excitement was great but just before Sir Stanley appeared Simon and his fellow Brits informed their American cousins exactly who the principal guest was – they had never heard of him nor, at that time, did they know anything about football (i.e. soccer to them!) and were hugely disappointed and completely lost interest.

Our hometown of Chelmsford was one of those involved in the early days of twinning with towns in France (as if we have anything in common!). Simon, with his deputy Gunn, and the Head were invited to the civil reception in the town. High quality French wine was available in a wine tasting interlude and the idea was to taste it, swill it around the mouth and then spit it into the receptacle provided. This Hughes and Gunn did with the first tasting but with the next eight glasses they did not wish to waste the good wine! Within an hour they were well gone and had to slink away before anyone, including the Head, noticed their inebriation.

All Full Prefects including the Head Boy had to read the lessons in morning assembly. We normally had to do a stint for the week. It was pretty nerve wracking in front of hundreds of boys waiting for you to stumble, lose your place or generally make a complete mess of the whole thing, Hughes had to read out and repeat, several times, the phrase – "and he climbed on his ox and rode to Annas" Three times he had to say Annas and each time it came out sounding like "Arse" – the boys tittered and Hughes went red when he realised what he had done. The Head never said a word!

If reading the lesson was not nerve racking enough the Head Boy's most daunting task was to speak at the annual Old Boys' Dinner in the school hall – it still is in fact. In the 60s these dinners were far more raucous than they are today where the Head Boy is now treated with respect. The Head Boy had not only to cope with the worry of getting up on his feet but also to stay sober enough to do so due to the fact that he was normally plied with copious amounts of alcohol! There was always heckling in these early dinners and this one was no exception. At least it was a good test of character and taught one a lot about the art of public speaking – either you survived and knew that there would never be a worse situation to face in the future or you vowed never to get up and speak in front of an audience again. Hughes coped manfully for one so young and became an accomplished public speaker in his later life. The guest speaker was an Old Boy called Norman Fowler MP and later Cabinet Minister. He started off by saying he was not a worthy enough speaker to address such an august gathering to which some wag in the audience shouted, "Well go home now as it's September!"

After the dinner Hughes was congratulated by many of the Old Boys who insisted on buying him a drink. Needless to say after more than eight pints he had to leave the hall rather quickly and deposit his dinner in the rose bushes outside the Head's study. The following summer the roses looked more beautiful than ever!

27

WELCOME TO THE PREFECT'S ROOM!

The following is a spoof article originally written for publication by the school magazine in 1967. It was rejected!

"Good morning and welcome to a short tour of the King Edward VI Grammar School in Chelmsford. I am Cynthia Penrose from the BBC. I shall be visiting the Prefect's Room in the oldest part of the school building that was opened in 1892. Now in 1967 this particular room is no longer used as a classroom and is where the Prefects, who largely maintain the discipline in the school, are allowed to spend their private study periods outside of lessons, instead of joining the rest of the sixth formers who have to use the Library for this type of studying.

There are two types of Prefect at the school. There are ten Full Prefects, which includes the Head Boy and his Deputy and the four Captains of the Houses plus four other specially selected senior boys. There are about fifteen sub prefects who are largely responsible for the discipline of the younger pupils and with this they are supported by the Masters. You can easily pick out the two different types of Prefect as the Full version wear essentially black ties with a neat yellow, green and blue narrow cross stripe (apparently this doubles as the Old Chelmsfordians' tie) but the Sub prefects wear a red tie with black and white narrow cross stripes.

The boys in this room are the "crème de la crème" of the school and set to go off to University in the next year or so and in the future to become the captains of industry or highly ranked civil servants or even professional academics. So as we move into the room let's see what these private study sessions are like and how these highly talented schoolboys settle into the daily grind of study for their forthcoming A-levels!

I'll just open the door and go in. Good God what was that! It's a tennis ball and it's just hit the wall above my head and bounced around the room."

"Sorry about that," shouted the tall young man in the middle of the room.

"That's all right – can I ask what you are doing?"

"Yes I was practising my forward defensive from Little's leg break and I got a leading edge – no harm done I hope!"

"No I'm fine thanks – now let me see, in front of me is a large bookshelf with cubby holes and this is where the boys keep their books. Ah! Chaucer and King Lear now this one here is a bit more modern – it's a Penguin book – Oh it's "Lady Chatterley's Lover". Good grief this is in a state. Let me open it. This is difficult as quite a few of the pages are stuck together. Also quite a few pages have an inky cross at the bottom and some of the text is underlined – Oh I see … I'd better put it back.

Now the room is a sizeable old classroom with three windows along the wall in front of me and in front of that is a long table with chairs all round. To my left and along one wall is a series of old armchairs and these carry on along the end wall. To my right are the bookshelves full of those, how should I say, various books.

Oh sorry. Everyone, I've just tripped over the feet of a boy who is asleep in the armchair and the Head Boy has pointed out that this is his Deputy who apparently had a bit of a session at the Lion and Lamb last night and is not feeling too well and has already been sick twice since morning assembly. The Head Boy has returned to the table to my right. I'll just follow him and see what he's doing. Oh it's Shove Ha'penny and he's apparently in the middle of a match in the Prefect's room championship. Well I have to say he's doing rather well.

I'm just passing the batsman who is making exaggerated forward defensive strokes and he's just told me he's practising his defence for Saturday's match, as he's the school's cricket captain.

There are a host of magazines here on the table and one suspects these will be the "Spectator" or something similar. I'll just turn these two over. Now what have we got? Ah "Playboy" and "Mayfair" - very nice. There's today's copy of the Sun and it's open at page three. Right, I'll just move on along the table. Ouch! Ah the tennis ball again it's just caught the back of my leg. Oh dear it's laddered my tights. It's all right thanks. Sorry everyone, the batsman has just apologised for another false shot! Now we have a boy here reading the bawdy Miller's Tale by Geoffrey Chaucer of course. Are you studying this for A-level? No? He's shaking his head everyone. Now next to him is a smart young man writing away furiously. Can I see what you are writing? "Dear June, I still have your knickers in my satchel…" Oops better leave that I think!

Now the Head Boy has finished his game and is with me and he's just asked if I would like to join him outside in the corridor as out there we have the school bell which the Prefects press at the end of each forty minute lesson so the masters and pupils know when that lesson has come to an end and the next one is due to start.

I've just looked at my watch, Simon, and it says two minutes to go, should we not wait?"

"No Cynthia we often ring it a minute or so early just to wind up one of the masters who is the sort of Deputy, Deputy Head and it really annoys him when his English lessons are cut short!"

"I see – right then let's just step over your Deputy here who's still asleep. Oh sorry – I've just tripped over his foot and woken him up. Sorry!"

"Hello darlin' did I pick you up last night?"

"Ian it's Cynthia Penrose from the BBC."

"Oh sorry love."

"We're outside now and here's the button to press and I've been given the honour. Right there we go! We'll stand here for a minute and see what happens. Here come some of the younger boys out of the classroom next to the Prefect's Room, good grief aren't they noisy! Ah here comes the Deputy Head Boy who is running and holding his hand across his mouth, where is he going? I see … straight into the toilets! Just coming along the corridor is one of the masters in his flowing black gown. Who's this Simon?"

"Shit! It's Isaiah Lee – he's the one we wind up."

"Hughes is that you again how many more times have I got to bloody tell you that the lessons last forty minutes not thirty eight, that's the fourth time this week! Oh sorry Miss I didn't see you there."

"Sir this is Cynthia Penrose from the BBC, we invited her to ring the bell."

"Oh dear, everyone, I seem to have upset Mr Lee as he's just stormed off. Well there we have it - the life in and around the Prefect's room – not quite what I was expecting but interesting nonetheless. This is Cynthia Penrose saying goodbye to you all from Chelmsford, Goodbye and I return you to the studio for the shipping forecast."

28

I HEAR THE SOUNDS OF DISTANT DRUMS!

The long summer days of 1966 drift into July, the World Cup has started. The exams are all finished. The O-level and A-level papers have been sent off for marking and those affected will have to wait until late August to get their results. For the O-level students it was a case of securing at least five passes so as to get into the sixth form, four or less and you had to go into The Remove and sit some subjects again just before Christmas. For those taking A-levels it was a question of grades to get that place at university or colleges or grades to secure that job at the Bank or Insurance Company. No one had yet invented gap years and National Service had ended a few short years before!

Some boys, therefore, were leaving the school forever having been there for at least five years. There were some enterprising young men named

Pearl, Spurling and Rippingale (all Prefects) who had a cunning plan and roped in some of their mates to serve as their trusted lieutenants. They had decided they would disrupt final assembly traditionally held in mid-afternoon on the last day of the school year. They carefully wrote out their plans and each had a copy. During the night before and in the early hours they easily got into the school and set up their ingenious interruption. Spurling was caught by his parents just as he was about to leave home and had to return to bed leaving Pearl and Rippingale to carry out the plan's next phase.

During the day of the assembly a message went round the school. Pupils would go up to each other all the time "Psst – don't sing the second verse of the hymn today, pass it on!" And "Psst – listen out for the crunch when the Head and the other Masters walk across the stage in the Hall, someone has dropped sugar on the floor and there are some dead fish in the drawer of the Head's desk on stage so you might see them all wondering what on earth the smell is!"

We Prefects heard it all but decided we could do nothing, or more likely chose not to. The planners remained anonymous at that time.

At the appointed hour the five hundred or so boys filed into the Hall for the final assembly. Chairs were provided for all on the ground floor and upstairs in the balcony there were fixed seats and these were filled by the first and second years. Downstairs there was a strict order from the front to back. The Head Boy and the Senior Prefects sat in the front row facing the stage, the Sub Prefects filled up the rest of the front row and the row behind. Then came the sixth formers, then the fifth and so on.

Our English and Music Master, John Jordan, sat at the organ expensively purchased a year or so before. There was a hubbub with the excitement of this being the end of term and the school year. We waited to hear the crunch and any reaction on the stage from where the Masters in their black gowns would look down on us. This all seemed a bit of a jape but we Sub Prefects had to show responsibility and went round quietening everyone down.

Mr Jordan played a rhapsody of some sort as the Masters came in led by the Head. There was a crunching noise but not as loud as we and the gang might have liked. A titter went round the Hall. There was no immediate reaction to any unpleasant odour and the smelly fish in the drawer might have been a "red herring"!!

First up came the non-singing of the second verse of the hymn. A few of the swots and gentle souls amongst the boys and, of course, the Prefects and the staff were, indeed, the only ones singing.

There was no laughing by those who kept quiet but some of the Masters looked angrily at we Prefects as if it was our fault.

Next up was the Head Boy who walked up onto the stage and to the lectern to read today's "lesson" from the Bible. More tittering as he crunched his way across the stage.

He started less than confidently, "Today's lesson is taken from the first Apostle of Paul the Epistle to the Corinthians Chapter 13" – more tittering. More frowns from the Masters. The Head was oblivious to all this as he had one final check of his notes and to the end of year speech he always gave. He had been at the school for seventeen years and invariably said the same thing each year so he was probably worrying unnecessarily.

The Head Boy got through Chapter 13 unscathed and finished with "Hope Faith and Charity and the greatest of these three is Charity."

The Head Boy crunched his way back to his seat. Yet more titters and some of the Full Prefects stood up and ordered "Quiet".

The Head rose to his feet and picked up the typed pages and started to read his speech. He had just got into his stride when suddenly there was a loud ringing from behind the resplendent curtains at the back of the stage. It sounded like a very loud alarm clock of the type common at the time that woke you up always too early in the mornings.

The Head stopped and looked round confused. "Noggs" Newman stood up and started trying to find the parting in the curtains looking like Eric Morecambe who always did this for a laugh on his show.

Other Masters joined in and the school started to laugh. A crescendo of murmuring and giggling went round. The Prefects did not know what to do, whether to join in with the laughter or calm down the throng.

Suddenly as "Noggs" found the exit to the store area at the back of the stage there was this loud noise. Boom! Boom! Boom! Boom! On and on it went. The Hall was in uproar. The Head sat down, bemused. Most of the Masters were now behind the curtain. The Deputy Head came down from the stage towards the Prefects, his face angry.

"Get the boys back to their form rooms - immediately!" he stammered purple with rage.

We started to comply. We opened the double doors from the Hall into the canteen. The Catholic and Jewish boys, who had to miss the religious part of the proceedings but had come in to hear the Head's speech, had already opened one of the doors. We ushered them out of the way and led all the boys out. Still we could hear a terrible commotion at the back of the stage but the "Booms" had eventually stopped.

The Full and Sub Prefects saw the boys to their rooms and then went back to the Prefect's room. Only the perpetrators knew who they were and we guessed they might be with us in the room. Some hinted they might have done the sugar and the fish but it was all rather confusing. "Isaiah" Lee, he with the one eye higher than the other, was having none of this and stormed into our sanctuary then sent us back to our form rooms,

The form masters regaled us with threats of keeping us behind at the school until the culprits owned up. An hour went by and no one from my form clearly had any idea who had done this and really had no idea of what had, in fact, really happened. Masters came and went and scurried everywhere.

The Head Boy found out that someone had rigged an alarm clock timed to go off when the perpetrators thought the religious part of the proceedings had come to an end and the Head was in full flow. They had been spot on! The alarm bell triggered a tray full of marbles and other spherical objects to gently tilt forward and drop one by one onto a kettledrum placed precisely underneath, hence the "Boom!" "Boom!"

Word of this soon got round to all the boys. Everyone was in fits but as more than an hour ticked by we all became more quiet and reflective on the genius of the perpetrators of the "crime".

After about an hour and a quarter we were allowed home. The gang were never traced that day and the Head never got to read his speech; he probably kept it and read it in 1967! Only recently have the guilty eventually owned up.

29

AN INCH MAKES ALL THE DIFFERENCE!

It's June 1968 and we are in the middle of flower power era and the first "Summer of Lurve" but not quite so prevalent in an all-boys school but many of us were now "courting" strongly.

One Saturday afternoon saw Sports Day arrive. The four "Houses" of Strutt, Tindal, Mildmay and Holland were all vying to become "Cock House" but Strutt, as throughout most of the sixties, were already wooden-spoonists that year having declined steadily from being **the** House of the fifties. Holland as usual flattered to deceive but were more in contention this year due to the fact that Hughes of Holland, when he was Head Boy the year before, had made sure that when any new boys with any particular sporting talents were allocated to Houses, Holland got first choice. Thus all the good sportsmen joined that

House - none more notable than Chris Flint who had arrived in 1966.

As Vice House Captain of Mildmay I would be heavily involved in organising my troops during the afternoon of the Sports Day. Although a reasonable athlete I would not be called upon that day to perform. Luckily our House Captain, David "Dickie" Dawson was an accomplished runner. His best distance was 440 yards but our Sports Field was so small that the four lane grass track was only 330 yards, yet he was certain to bring home the spoils in not only this but also the 220. I nearly made the 100 and was on standby but our man arrived to save me the trouble so there I was rounding up the boys from the different year groups for a team talk.

I saw "Dickie" going through his warm up routine when he was approached by one of the younger boys from the second year. This boy reported that his older brother had a groin strain and would not be able to make the event. "Dickie" checked his records and saw the older boy had been roped in for the Hop, Step and Jump. When "Dickie" saw the event he knew the strain might well be more in the head than the groin because the school's best two athletes, already capped by Essex, were in that event.

Martin "Paddy" Mulqueen and Keith Pepperell were not only the best Hop, Step and Jumpers in the school but also in the whole of Essex in their age group. They were so good that our Sports Master Mr Pike had been worried that our sand pit into which they were to jump was not far enough away from the jumping board! The groin strain boy saw no point in giving up his Saturday afternoon, which he could better spend with his girl friend as opposed to picking up no more than third in the H, S and J!

"Dickie" came over and told me of the missing man, "We're one down for the Triple Jump and that means we will not stand a chance of even one House point. If we could get third it would add two to our year's total and even fourth would get us a point and the way the House competition is going this year every point is vital. Would you do it?"

I almost instinctively said, "Not a chance," but then I thought of my responsibility to Mildmay and that we were the defending "Cock House" from 1967 the competition won under "Gus" Gunn's leadership. Again I had been his Vice (second in command has been a theme throughout my life thus far!) and we had truly taken over Strutt's mantle as the House everyone wanted to beat.

So I found the master in charge and informed him of the change to the personnel in the event. I had brought along some kit just in case and put this on.

The H, S and J was not until just before the end of the day. The 4 x 100 sprints were all that were left after my event. The cinder run up and the pit were right at the top end of the Sports Field. With Paddy or Keith likely to break a long standing school record it was disappointing that only a few spectators made their way to the sand pit.

Unlike today hardly any parents came along to watch such events in the sixties but Ron Pepperell was there to watch his son. I knew Ron well as he played cricket twice a year against my Dad's team for whom I scored and sometimes played. We had a chat and he was nervous for Keith as the rivalry between Keith and Paddy was immense not just on this day but for a place in the Essex team.

We stood around the cinder run up and checked in with the steward running the event. We were told we had three jumps each and he would be checking the white board to make sure we didn't overstep. Keith and Paddy were doing their normal pre-competition routines. Carefully marking out their runs and leaving a marker by the side of the track. They did a whole host of stretches. I ran around looking like I knew what I was doing and trying to remember how they did this thing on the telly.

There were some jumping icons at that time what with Mary Bignal-Rand and Lynn Davies both winning Olympic gold in Tokyo in 1964. I remembered some of Welshman Davies's poses not that they were anything like we get today. I would have done the rhythmic handclapping warm up before my go if only it had been invented by 1968. But to do it in front of the equivalent of two men and a dog it might not carry the same motivational strength!

Talking of the crowd, apart from Ron, the judge/master, a boy to measure the jumps, and a few of the senior House officials my girlfriend Chrissie Sharp had arrived and found me stripped and ready for action – for the H, S and J of course! She thought it highly amusing that I was to attempt this feat. A few friends such as Smith and Brunwin (Tindal), Flint and Hollebon (Holland) and Brazendale (Strutt) eventually arrived to cheer on their men. Keith was Holland, Paddy was Strutt, but I forget who was from Tindal and then me from Mildmay.

"You'll never make the pit," said Smith to me – and to think he was to become my best man when I got married!

"Hey Chrissie," said Flint, for whom I was to be Best Man, "why don't you give his legs a massage then he might reach the pit!" Much guffawing and embarrassment followed this.

"I hope you had a quiet night last night," chipped in Hollebon, and so it went on.

The Tindal man went first. He made the pit and there was a little applause. Paddy was next. He walked back to his plimsoll being used as his mark. As is the "professional" jumper's wont, he makes to move off about seven times but holds back - apparently it's all to do with psyching themselves up … really?

Paddy was off down the cinder track. Now this might have looked straightforward in Tokyo but on Westfields in Chelmsford it was another matter. The track undulated where footprints had worn it away and it was U-shaped with the dip in the middle. It was as if someone had dug a little gully for the water to drain away. But this gully was caused by years of use and because no one ever raked it over or repaired it. So, a twisted ankle was always likely and you made sure you stepped carefully.

Off Paddy went Hop…. Step and oh my god! – What a jump! Two inches from the end of the pit and he may have come down a little early to make sure he did not land on the grass.

Keith was next to go. Same routine, same result. Landing almost in the same place as Paddy.

Then it was my turn. I only knew how to mark out a bowler's run up for cricket and did much the same here except that when I did it I was far too close to the jumping board so I had to go back further to a Freddie Trueman length. I marked the track with the sole of my plimsoll (no running spikes for me, the school did give them out to boys but you had to be better than just "good" at athletics – It was a bit like cricket, if you were a top six batsman in the batting order you got a "box" of your own but if you batted seven to eleven you had to get your own, borrow or chance going into bat without one!)

Anyway, back to the runway! I might not have the technique for this event but I could sprint. I landed my right foot about a yard behind the take off board and went into the three phases. It all went like clockwork as I had the speed to get through the last one and that was the key. I landed in the sand and jumped up. A white flag (handkerchief actually) so it was a legal jump. It was a wonder the steward spotted where my foot landed as I was so far behind the board!

I got out of the sand so the steward, assisted by the master, could get on with his measuring. I looked at my friends and they looked aghast at my effort. They walked over and looked into the sandpit to make sure the sand spurting everywhere hadn't misled them and to see how good my effort was. They then looked at me and I looked back in that sort of cocky teenage way. Then the boys looked at Chrissie as if to say, "Do you believe that?" – she looked even more smug than me but eventually came over and said, "I didn't realise you would be that good, where did that come from."

"It's all down to technique," I said gloating and lying.

The boys then gathered themselves and started making derogatory remarks about my newly acquired prowess making sure I was soon brought down to earth.

Yes, it was a good jump but it was ten feet behind Keith and Paddy. The Tindal man who was no slouch was just behind me by about an inch. However, he had succumbed to the cinder track curse and turned his ankle when attempting that first jump and announced that he was unable to carry on. I had beaten him by an inch!

Such was my euphoria I took no notice who won the battle of the greats but they both stayed in the pit so it was close. There was no point taking my second and third jumps as I would never reach the other two and anyway I would rest on my laurels!

Even to this day I have my third place certificate and this position duly chalked up my two House points to go towards our grand total. The length of the jump is recorded as 38 feet and 8 inches on my certificate and the world record in 1968 was over 55 feet so only about six yards short then!

The day of the final assembly of the year arrived and it was then that the Head announced the results and the total points for the House competition which involved hockey, cricket, football, sport standards, sports day, examination results, disciplinary penalty point reductions and so on.

The Head gives Strutt's lowly score to groans from the Struttites and laughs from the rest. Holland, through Hughes's conniving, were in third place, with a better points total than in recent times. The Head then read out the total points for Tindal and then for Mildmay – Mildmay were "Cock House" by ONE POINT. Quite unbelievable!

A twisted ankle for the Tindal man and my prodigious fluke had seen us home, so that I could leave the school with Mildmay, the dregs in 1960 when I joined, now double "Cock House" in 1967 and 1968.

As we all moved away from the school but remained friends, the "in" joke with my friends remained that they consistently reminded me of what a difference an inch makes!

What was an amusing coincidence was that the number one in the UK charts on June 22nd 1968, the day for the Sports, was Jumpin' Jack Flash by the Rolling Stones!

(In tribute to Martin "Paddy" Mulqueen who died tragically whilst climbing in 2007)

30

SCHOOLBOY PRANKS? – WELL IT SEEMED FUNNY AT THE TIME

End of school year pranks were more often than not a hoot such as with the aforementioned marbles falling on the drum disrupting the final assembly.

Some, however, would seem funny at the time but would have dire consequences and in one instance a potential tragedy.

Towards the end of one school year we were all suddenly kept in our classrooms. Prefects were put in charge of the classes and the teachers went around the school building checking on all the wash areas then they returned to the classrooms and relieved the prefects. A short inquisition then ensued and we found out what the fuss was all about. In the new toilets there was always bars of soap. They were never used that much as one might expect in a boy's school but on this particular morning one horrific find was made. As a boy picked up a bar and was about to lather his hands he saw little slivers of metal protruding from the soap. He looked more closely and could see they were razor blades broken in half, long ways, and pushed into the soap so that they just protruded.

The boy took the soap to his form master and this prompted the flap to search other potential targets. Fortunately there were none. What could possibly possess a boy or boys to contemplate such a thing? There was just this one bar and we shuddered to think what might have happened if this boy had not spotted the danger.

The culprit or culprits were never caught but you wonder how, over 40 years later, they could possibly be proud of what they did.

In the mid sixties one jape was very well engineered and highly amusing at the time but had a sad ending with the loss for a master of one of his most treasured possessions.

A group of fifth formers some of whom were leaving at the end of the summer term had decided to complete an elaborate prank. W.R. "Jake" Jackson was the popular history teacher and an old boy of the school, having been the Head Boy some years before. Being Boarding House master and with a flat on the school premises he kept his car in the car park behind the boarding House. He was the proud owner of a small, black 1930s Austin Seven.

The boys met in the dead of night on a July evening prior to the last day of term. They were easily able to get into "Jake's" car and slip the hand brake off and then push the car up the small ramp into the corridor leading to the quadrangles in the middle of the school. The corridors built in the 1890s were much wider than one would see today so the narrow car passed easily along them. The boys pushed it past the larger quadrangle and on to the next, smaller one. They carefully manoeuvred the car down the two feet drop by using planks as ramps.

They were now directly behind the two-storey block between the two quadrangles that housed the Staff Room on the ground floor with a science lab and another classroom above. One boy managed to get up onto the roof above the science lab and set up a pulley system and dropped a rope down to his accomplices. Those below had lifted the bonnet and ingeniously, and with a lot of knowledge for 16 year olds of how a car was put together, unscrewed, if that's the right word, the whole engine mounting and fastened it onto the rope and then hoisted it using the pulley so it just dangled from the roof of the building.

There it was left to be discovered in the morning. Unfortunately, the typical British summer took over and it rained for some hours before dawn.

Once discovered the whole school must have filed past at some time during the day to look at and admire the ingenuity of the conspirators. Much like the Gunpowder Plot the perpetrators were soon rounded up or gave themselves up. They were summarily dealt with by the Head who suspended them all. Some probably did not care as they were leaving anyway but it would still be put on their school report and record.

Poor "Jake" did get the engine back however, with the combination of rain damage and, in those days, almost immediate rusting plus the fact that 30 year old cars do not react too well to having their engines removed, the car never went on the road again. This was not what the boys had in mind but what seemed to us all a great wheeze fizzled out into something rather sad especially to the very popular "Jake".

...

Alongside this regrettable prank an even worse one was to follow a couple of years later and it was to have a similar unfortunate outcome.

Some masters are disliked, some became role models for us all and yet some just irritated us and we just want to take the mickey out of them. The idea of one group of sixth formers was to inconvenience one such master who was a little weak but to most of us seemed a decent chap. The group had some grievance or just wanted to have what they thought would be a laugh by disabling the man's Vauxall Viva.

Through their science lessons they had discovered that sugar in petrol causes a car engine to stop working so they decided to pour some sugar obtained from the school canteen through the petrol cap and wait for him to splutter to a stop at the school gates when he eventually went home.

Unfortunately the boys had not paid full attention in their science lessons or read further on in the text books because, if they had done so, they would have discovered that the sugar mixed with the petrol would cause the engine to cease up completely. This is what happened in this case and the master was never even able to start it up and the car was a write-off. The boys were never caught nor owned up.

...

Once the new school hall was in place in the mid sixties we had delivery of a new and very expensive organ and in John Jordan we had the most wonderful organist to take charge of it. He was later to go on to be Head of Music at Chelmsford Cathedral and even played at the Festival of Remembrance at the Royal Albert Hall in front of the Queen.

I fondly remember him practising and tuning it – I am not a classical music person but this was truly wonderful.

In my House, Mildmay, we had twin boys who were then in the second year when I was Vice House Captain. I knew them well as they were good sportsman and I was in charge of the junior House sports' teams.

Suddenly one day our Head Boy told the Prefects that these brothers had taken concentrated sulphuric acid from the Chemistry Lab and opened the top of the organ and tipped the acid inside, they had been caught and their parents called in. I could not believe it of these two likeable boys from a good home with supportive parents. The damage was not as bad as it might have been and the parents paid for the repairs and the organ was fine. The two boys had all privileges withdrawn which of course included their School and House sports. I am sure they will be able to recall to this day what they did and I wonder what they feel like now?

...

Now that we take time to look back, the boys who committed these acts of vandalism and even physical harm have probably become fathers themselves and may even be grandfathers today. What would they think of their offspring doing things like this?

Not particularly proud moments for a proud school.

31

HEALTH AND SAFETY? – IT'S NOT BEEN INVENTED YET!

One would expect leading Grammar Schools, in particular, to have high levels of Health and Safety even in the 1960s when such matters were not of the same importance as some authorities wish to give them today. The reality was that KEGS was no different from anywhere else in that it had its fair share of health and safety issues.

It had the very tragic collapse of Max Pemberton at the end of an athletics race and no doubt today the school might have been taken to task about the lack of first aid or in the area of due care in making largely unfit boys over extend themselves.

There were other incidents that occurred in the 60s that would also have caused more of an outcry nowadays.

...

WHERE THE BEE ....

One of the worst fears that we had was for the boys who played at our home ground for the cricket elevens. It could also be dangerous for parents to spend summer's afternoons and evenings watching their son play for the school.

Our main sports field was Newfields some half mile or so from the school. It was a field large enough to have two cricket squares and outfields with a rickety wooden pavilion between the two. In the winter it had three football pitches and they became two hockey pitches after Christmas. In order to get to the field, which was behind a line of large private houses along the main road to Broomfield, we had to pass through some ornamental gates and alongside the long gardens of two of the houses. A vet called Mr Newsome whose two boys went to the school in the 50s and 60s owned the one on the right.

With a clear liking for animals Mr Newsome's passion also extended to bee keeping and these were housed right at the end of his garden, which almost reached the boundary of the main cricket pitch.

As we played on Saturday afternoon and early evening, we would often still be playing until about 7. At about 6 the bees would be making their way home after a hard day's graft and their well-defined flight path went straight across, at right angles to, the wickets on the main cricket square. We always had to warn the opposition of possible interference if one of their fielders crossed the path of a bee in making a stop in the field, if they were going for a catch of course we hoped the bee would attack them!

One day Dick Cronin our opening fast bowler was steaming in from the pavilion end. Cronin had thick wavy hair and just as he delivered one of his fast away swingers he suddenly ran off towards long leg swishing at his head and ruffling his hair. Expletives abounded and eventually he came to a stop but it took a few seconds for us to realise that this was not some elaborate appeal for a catch or lbw or celebration of a wicket but an attempt to get a bee out of his curls. He survived!

Not quite so lucky was a spectator on another occasion. My friend, Rob Ketley, was playing on the other pitch behind the pavilion for the Under 15s. I was away with the first team. This is the same Rob Ketley, three years my junior but who lived round the corner from me, who put a cricket ball through the largest window in our house during one of my coaching (!) sessions the Friday afternoon before we were due to go on holiday early the following day. Our Dads had to hastily buy and fit a new pane and it took them well into that evening!

Anyway Mr Ketley came to watch the latter stages of his son's match after tea on a Saturday. As he walked round the first team boundary at just after 6 he met a Newsome bee and it stung his face. No sooner had he walked to where Rob was playing than he suffered an anaphylactic reaction and suddenly he looked like the monster from the lagoon as his face swelled up grotesquely. Someone rushed him off to hospital and he was successfully treated and recovered within a day or so. It did not do him any lasting damage and he is still going strong well into his 90s!

...

I TOLD YOU GERMANS COULDN'T PLAY CRICKET!

Our fourth year exams were over but in those days we had to see out the rest of the summer term attending school but we were allowed to enjoy ourselves a little. This particular year we had a visit from some similar aged children on an exchange from Germany. Of course this would have been July 1964 and so less than 20 years after the war had come to an end. We were philosophical about these things but some resented the presence of the Germans especially if their families had lost a loved one during the hostilities, also the Luftwaffe had repeatedly bombed Chelmsford in view of its, then, manufacturing industry.

We got on well with the students and one in particular who was an enormous boy called Helmut with huge shoulders and a head that was as square as they come: if there ever was such a thing as an archetypical German then he was it, well to us anyway who were brought up on the Germans depicted in our comics!

One afternoon we were playing an impromptu game of cricket on the outfield at Newfields. We managed to find some old kit in the pavilion but only a bat, ball and some stumps. We had to explain to Helmut the rudiments of the game – "Stodge" was not so interested. His Dad was a policeman and had served in the war and the dislike of Germans may have been strong in their house. "Stodge" was adamant that being German this chap would not take it seriously and be useless anyway so he didn't wish to play.

Steve Cawley offered to serve up a few "donkey drops" for Helmut to hit when it was his turn to bat. I was in my usual place behind the stumps as wicket keeper but had no hat, gloves, box or pads as protection. Cawley served up a genial long hop so Helmut could blast the ball where he liked. He took so long making up his mind that he left it to the last second to hit and when he did it should have sailed away for four runs behind the wicket. Unfortunately my face was in the way and the hard cricket ball hit me flush on my right cheek. It glanced away and just left a nick on my face and a little bit of blood. Helmut was beside himself but as we all do at these times laughed initially as much through shock as anything about what he had done. "Dummkopf" he kept saying about himself. I kept saying I was OK and not hurt but deep down I was feeling "Bloody Germans, just don't invade Poland again that's all!"

I felt all right for the rest of the day. I didn't even need a plaster but the next morning I woke up with a severe headache and when I looked into the bedroom mirror my eyes were like those of Chi Chi the famous giant panda featured in the news at that time. Mum did not know whether to laugh or cry at first but told me to stay at home which was just as well as I could not see much!

The day after this it was still just as bad so I stayed at home again. At about 4.30 in the afternoon the doorbell rang and it was my friend Nige Ottley. When I opened the door he looked shocked when he saw my face and typically laughed then apologised. He was concerned about me and had been aware of the injury so he dropped in to check I was all right.

He also came with some great news. In English that day our English master John Jordan had eulogised about one of his pupils who had excelled himself in the recent exam sat by the 101 boys in the 4th year. Despite being in Set 3, and therefore of third quartile performance normally, this pupil had come 3rd out of 101. It was due to a brilliant (his words!) essay explaining cricket to an American (!) and after this eulogy he got to the naming of the pupil – it was ... Little!

Apparently the boys then laughed and Jordan lost his temper for a moment but refrained from his normal chalk throwing. They had to explain to him that I was off sick. So here was Nige with this news. I would be in Set 1 next year with Mr "Isaiah" Lee a bit of a daunting thought amongst all this euphoria.

From then on I was Mr Jordan's pin up boy. Coincidentally I met him once by chance in the outside toilet of the Plough near Chelmsford railway station a couple of years after the exam feat. There were three other chaps in there when John saw me and said "Oh my dearest chap how lovely to see you," in his upper class accented way. The other three chaps in the toilet quickly shook off the drips and soon got out of there!

...

BOMB ALERT!

The Chemistry lab was a dangerous place. Bunsen burners were attached to gas pipes sticking up out of the benches. Concentrated Sulphuric Acid was on the shelves together with a host of other acids and dangerous substances.

Thirty or so boys might be in the lab at any one lesson and could not be adequately supervised but generally they acted with some responsibility. One boy did get hydrochloric acid spilt onto his hands and there was some burning to his skin. Today his parents might have commenced a lawsuit against the school or used someone such as *unlikelycompoforyou.com* to get some money for their next holiday but not in those days!

Days We'll Remember All Our Lives

The boy bore a grudge though against the Chemistry teachers and even the School itself. He studied his chemistry text books and got another book out of the library. He decided he would make a bomb (well a large "banger" firework really!) and let it off somewhere relatively safe around the school but this would be his "revenge".

He was able to relieve the chemistry lab of some essential ingredients and set about following in the footsteps of Guy Fawkes and his mates.

He of course would not know if his "device" would work until he lit the "touch paper" but he chose the site of the outside toilets as somewhere suitable for his protest. Having carefully manufactured his bomb, he made sure the toilets were empty and went into a cubicle and set up his "device" but he had miscalculated on the length of the fuse and at this late hour almost had second thoughts as he now realised he might not be able to make his escape before the explosion. However, he took a chance!

He struck his match and at arms length lit the thing and shot out of the cubicle and out through the door to the toilets and he just made it, as there was this most almighty explosion. But it was only the reverberation of the noise that made any impact and there was no damage apart from some light burning to the tiled floor.

He did not think he needed to telephone a warning to the School to dramatise his act of "revenge" but had it been in the 70s when bombs were going off all over the UK he might have thought differently!

Nowadays on hearing the "explosion" the School might well ring for armed back up, the anti-terrorist squad, S.W.A.T. or the SAS and seal off the area for days and carry out forensic tests but in the 60s the culprit was soon apprehended and got a good whack for his trouble.

Who knows, he might have become a nuclear physicist but then again a safe breaker or something even more sinister…!

...

HOCKEY? ISN'T THAT JUST A GAME FOR CISSIES!

As already mentioned the school played hockey instead of football after Christmas and, bearing in mind nearly all the boys had never played the game before they went to the school, we did produce some excellent teams and players who went on to play at a very high level, not least my contemporaries Ian Brown and Simon Hughes.

In February 1967 I was nursing this thigh strain and was unable to play football but with less use of those muscles required for hockey I asked the second eleven captain, Keith Lacey, if he might need someone to make up the team for Saturday.

As it happened he did, so I would be able to give my now nearly mended thigh a good workout.

This was my only game for the school and we won! Bitter sweet success though for the aforementioned skipper, Lacey. During a scramble in the goal area following a short corner he got a whack on the eyebrow for his troubles and went down like a sack of potatoes. We gathered round him and he assured us he was fine. He did not look like it though as his eye looked like one of Henry Cooper's after one of his renowned "Referee stopped fight because of cut eye" bouts in the 60s.

Lacey had an immense cut right across his eyebrow and I have never seen one as large and deep as that before or since. He recovered. We footballers often thought hockey players were a bit girly, it being a girls' game to us, but this proved it wasn't and Keith showed how tough he was!

House hockey matches were titanic struggles where good players came up against bad and we all came up against the psycho who just went round trying to hit you rather than the ball. Then our games were played on grass so the play was much slower than on the modern all-weather pitches but shin pads were often not enough to protect you from the psychos. Most of us did, however, often take the opportunity to settle some old scores from playground disagreements.

Our masters, notably Ken Newman, kept fairly good control but the mishap to little Graham King was something no one could prevent. He was hit flush in the face by the hockey ball during a house match and knocked out completely. He, too, recovered. He was not quite so lucky on another occasion when he was laid out cold when being hit during a Games session by a flying baseball bat as he stood next in line to go into bat when the boy in front set off for his home run, flung the bat backwards with no control, straight in Kingy's face! He had to spend some time in hospital.

...

Were these character-building events that made us all aware of what life could be like? Does sport mirror life itself? No action was taken about any of these incidents, parents did not rush to the school to complain they just told their children to get up and get on with it. This was probably left over from the wartime experiences they had had. Today things might well be different!

32

GIRLS DON'T MAKE PASSES AT BOYS WEARING GLASSES

It was often said that boys don't make passes at girls wearing glasses but it was equally thought by boys in the 60s that the same applied to them should they have to wear glasses. Of course, glasses were either "National Health" ones, perhaps a quick buy in Woolworth's from their selection without having a proper test, or "designer" frames that were a choice of not very many and they made you look geeky!

Whether it was coincidence or not my eyesight suddenly worsened immediately after the German exchange student had hit me in the face with the cricket ball.

Even before that, though, I was having trouble reading the blackboard in class and embarrassingly once put my hand out to stop the 44A numbered bus when I actually thought it had the number I wanted namely, 43A. I was red in the face when I told the grumpy conductor that I had made a mistake.

Things had got worse after the cricket ball incident, so my Mum took me off aged 15 to see the new optician in town a kind and friendly man called Edmund Wilkes. I told him I was having difficulty when standing at the bus stop and reading the bus number as the vehicle approached. He comforted me by saying that it's when you can't see the bus coming that you really have to worry!

Anyway, I secured my new "designer" specs and they did indeed make me look like a geek or so I thought but needs must! I also secured a pair of even more unflattering unbreakable glasses for cricket. They were black rimmed with wired ends so they could be secured behind the ears so as not to fly off when you tried to hit a four or a six.

By the time I was 17 the glasses were deemed not suitable for socialising, more accurately called "going out trying to get off with women" - at least in my circle of friends. The problem was my eyesight in those two years had got significantly worse. So when, for example, I was going out with Linda M in 1966, I would sit through a film at the cinema only vaguely being able to see what was on the screen. We never got shown to the back row and I was never comfortable kissing with someone watching from behind me, so I could not embroil myself in snuggling up to Linda rather than watch the film that, quite frankly, gave me a headache as I strained to make out what was happening. I am not sure Linda ever knew about my myopia but she might have guessed something was wrong when I flagged a bus down at the bus stop where we had been having a good night kiss only to find, like before, I had misread the number.

Contact lens would have been an answer but they were not really openly available to the ordinary public at that time due to the exorbitant cost.

Even in February 1967 when I met Chrissie I was still without glasses when out on the town. Little did I know that she, too, was as myopic as me but equally vain! Our first two dates were "glasses–less" and then I arranged to meet her after school on the steps of the Public Library. I decided to take the plunge and come clean about the glasses. I saw her there with her friend and as I approached Chrissie suddenly recognised me, despite the glasses, but only when I was really close to her. Her friend excused herself with "You might have told me" – I thought she meant being told that I was a four-eyed geek but she really meant that Chrissie should have told her it was me that was approaching so she could move away before I got there. However, as it turned out, Chrissie had failed to recognise me probably as much to do with her myopia as my "changed" look!

Eventually Chrissie came clean that she did need glasses as well but generally continued to show her vanity in this regard for a number of years, really up until she learnt to drive in the 1970s.

Steve Little

During the 60s I did eventually succumb to the vanity of contact lens and what an experience that was! My main problem was with sport. I could wear my "unbreakables" for cricket but football is more macho and I looked more "geekish" than I did normally should I have to wear them on the pitch during a game. This would only normally be for evening games where there were no floodlights or dark December days when the light goes early. I did put them on in one game but the opposition gave me so much embarrassing stick that I vowed to get contact lens.

In those days the only choice was "hard lens" – the least comfortable nowadays. Due to the cost the optician always made you have a test run. I went to see Edmund Wilkes and he put the lens in and they were not too bad but I was blinking twenty to the dozen and my eyes watered a little. His task, however, for all his patients was for them to then go outside in the street in the middle of Chelmsford and walk round for an hour to see if they could live with the considerable discomfort at least until they got used to them.

Now in the optician's room there was not too much bright light and it was all artificial. I then went outside into the street having been told to come back in an hour.

As soon as I went outside the door the very bright sunshine almost knocked me over with its effect as I could barely open my eyes, which streamed with tears that ran down my face and I had to keep mopping them with my handkerchief.

Subjected to being out in the town on this busy Saturday morning, I dreaded meeting someone I knew as, to look at me, they might have thought someone close to me had passed away. I staggered up the main street and eventually settled on a corner of a bus shelter to hide away from the possible prying eyes of friends or just from the ordinary people in the street who had already given me a lot of strange looks!

Eventually the hour, one of the longest in my life was up and I staggered back to Mr Wilkes. Despite this horrendous trial I went ahead and have worn them ever since but gas permeable lens and disposable soft lens have made life easier but there were a lot of my contemporaries who were put off by their experiences in the "hour" and either stuck with their glasses or got on the wrong buses!!

33

TRAGEDY!

In eight years at the school there are so many exciting and amusing things that happened to brighten up the drudgery of school life but inevitably there were moments of great sadness.

In 1966 two boys died outside of school time. One was John B Pearce a 12 year old that died at home in his sleep. Another was Roger Barden, a sixth former, who was out sailing one weekend with two friends on the Thames when they capsized. Roger tried to swim to the shore to get help but drowned before he could get there. There was a sombre mood in the school following both tragedies.

A very popular pupil was Mick Aldridge but he died in his first year up at university. He had been Mildmay house captain and a fine footballer and cricketer. He, it was rumoured, had received a kick on his ankle at football in his mid teens whilst at the school and from that a cancerous growth had developed. He had his foot removed and an artificial one provided but, alas, the cancer spread to the rest of his body and he passed away shortly after leaving the school.

The fourth tragic event happened one sunny summer morning in1967.

During our time at the school "standards" were introduced into our athletics' curriculum. It was a worthy idea and generally successful. Yet it was to unwittingly contribute to the death of a young man.

For all athletics and field events that the school could provide, the sports masters set certain standards of times and distances in each event. There were Bronze, Silver and Gold and if you attained them you got 1, 2 or 3 points towards your House's grand total to decide who would be "Cock" House at the end of the school year.

A large number of us were fairly sporty and would aspire to the gold. The House masters and Captains and senior boys would cajole the less athletic, in particular, to at least get the 1 point for a bronze standard.

During "Games" lessons we would be encouraged to be supervised in all the events possible in an 80-minute session and strive to secure these points. The keen ones amongst us would pick up our points by doing these after school time and get our points on the board early on and then try for something better subsequently. A reasonable athlete would manage mainly gold.

Steve Little

One morning our group had double games for the first part of the school day. Some of us went up to the cricket nets on the sports field next to the school to practise and I was batting and "Stodge" Stoneham was bowling quickly at me. Back down the bottom part of the field was the 330-yard grass, four-lane track. The less sporty boys were there in their own group. Suddenly after a shout of "Go" the four runners set off. The staggered start accentuated the leader's position but he was yards ahead of the others even ignoring the stagger.

I stopped batting and said to Stodge "Bloody hell, who's that? He's running like the wind."

"It's Pemberton!" "Stodge" said in surprise. "I didn't know he could run so fast!"

With that we carried on with the cricket for about 10 minutes then it was time to go in to get changed and move on to our next lesson. The runners had completed their 330 sprints as far away from us as they could be at the bottom of the field near the main road.

We packed away the cricket gear but when we got to the changing rooms in the oldest part of the school buildings there was something going on. People were running around and shouting. What's up we asked? It's Pemberton he's collapsed and we think he's dead was the response. Disbelieving, we cricketers looked at each other with concern etched all over our faces. We just sat in the changing room shocked.

Eventually one of the masters came in and told us to cut along, as we were already late for our next lesson. Is it true, sir, about Max Pemberton we all asked? He confirmed that it was.

Word got round the school. Lessons were stopped as all the boys were told. Poor Max it seems had collapsed after his run having pushed himself beyond his normal limit. He, we later learnt, had been sick and choked on it and that was it. So quick!

The school was in shock. Although there was no such thing as local radio or 24-hour news coverage, the news of Max's death spread around the factories just down the road from the school. My uncle heard that it was a 17 year old and he, my dad and grandparents who I lunched with every day were pleased to see me turn up at my Nan's at one o'clock. They had delayed their return to work just to make sure I was all right

Chrissie heard about it that day at her school some two miles away. She knew that I would have been there in all probability and she was mightily relieved when I met her at the bus station after school that day.

At assembly first thing the next morning there was none of the usual noise and bustle. A Prefect read the poignantly chosen lesson with passion. The Head confirmed to us what we already knew and we bowed our heads and observed a minute's silence in Max's memory.

34

YES – BUT YOU HAVEN'T GOT A FORD MUSTANG!

During the 60s, unlike teenagers now, not many of us sought the thrill of buying our first car when we were 17 or more likely have it bought for us by Mum and Dad. In fact we were lucky if they had a car themselves and certainly it was unlikely that they would have a second car for us to borrow.

Of course, we walked, cycled or got the bus to school even from the age of 5 and always without the company of our parents. No 4x4s to the school gates for us!

However, as we approached 17 we could at least plan to learn to drive, sort out some lessons and then take our driving tests before we left the school. Many of our older friends had already passed their test and one or two even had regular access to a car.

Days We'll Remember All Our Lives

As my birthday was at the end of the school year in June I would be one of the last to learn to drive. Some of my close friends in the same school year had reached 17 many months before and had their full licence already. The pressure was on to get through the test as soon as possible.

On my 17th birthday in 1966 I did have my first drive of my Dad's rather cumbersome Hillman Minx, which had a steering column gear lever. It was not the best car to learn in and I'm not sure my Dad was all that keen to teach me so he was more than willing to pay for my lessons

Ian Brown had used, and passed with, a private tutor who was not attached to any of the Schools of Motoring and he put me onto him. The lessons were 15 shillings (75p) for 50 minutes whereas the Schools charged £1 for an hour.

I started learning with this chap in his Vauxhall Viva every Monday evening at 6 and started in September. This was excellently timed as I could fit this in after homework and before Dad and I left to watch Chelmsford City's first or second team who invariably played on Monday evenings through the winter.

One day my instructor turned up with his nose plastered up with bruising everywhere on his face. I asked if he had been in an accident and he said, "No, the husband came home early!"

By January I was deemed proficient enough to take my test. It was scheduled for 8.30 on a Monday morning but could I sleep the night before? No, of course not! Now with most of my friends having been tested already we knew which examiners were the ones we would wish to avoid. When I was told the name of mine I feared the worst, as he was the one who was deemed to be against schoolboy drivers and preferred to pass slow moving, old drivers. It poured with rain all the way round the test route and it was dark enough to drive with headlights on. I did not make a mistake but was "Failed" – the worst thing was to have to suffer the ribbing from my mates when I got back to school. My Dad was less than comforting by saying he was not surprised as he felt I drove on my brakes, although at that time I did not know quite what he meant.

You could not take your test until at least a month later so I put in for it as soon as I could and the test was right at the end of February in the late morning. My Mum gave me a note for school but no one else knew I was taking it. I just told my mates that I had to go to the dentist.

Fortunately I avoided the previous examiner and on a clear day had an incident filled 35 minutes. On the then Chelmsford bypass there is a section that has no overtaking for about half a mile. As I approached this section there was a milk float going about 5 mph just short of the double white lines. Do I overtake or sit like a lemon behind him for half a mile with half of Chelmsford on my tail? Do I risk exceeding the speed limit to get by or risk going over the double white lines? The confidence of youth saw me glide by well before the lines. Phew!

We immediately turned left at the next junction and were now on a road on a housing estate. I overtook a row of cars and then suddenly 50 yards ahead a Volkswagen Beetle pulled right out in front of me without looking and came straight towards me. Thankfully he stopped and I carried on, when I really should have stopped (as I was told by the examiner when we got to the end of test!). About 400 yards further on I went past a primary school and a football came over the wall and bounced right on the bonnet of my car! Neither the examiner nor I said anything but I then had to turn into a side road to carry out the three-point turn. I stalled mid way across the road but we had always been told that's no problem as long as you start the car again correctly, which I must have done because 10 minutes later I got my pink slip telling me I'd passed.

My instructor was delighted. Peculiarly the then insurance rules stated that the pupil could not then drive the car back to the school, or so my tutor said! The couple of miles from the test centre to the school were the most hair raising I can recall when he drove like a complete maniac breaking umpteen road traffic regulations on the way. It reminded me of that old phrase "Don't do as I do but do as I say"!

I was eager to tell all my mates I'd passed and waved my pink slip in the same way that Neville

Chamberlain waved that white sheet of paper when he came back from Munich all those years before.

No sooner was I back at the school than it was lunchtime and I had to be off to my Nan's. I deliberately delayed my arrival there so that my Dad, Granddad and Uncle Ken had gone back to work so I could delay telling them, more my Dad really just to wind him up. He was not all that complimentary about my driving and continually mentioned the "driving on brakes".

I delayed getting home after school so I knew my Mum and Dad would be home from work. When I went down the side of the house I slammed the side gate and cursed loudly for effect. I slammed the shed door and then the back door and had a grim set face as I arrived in the living room.

"What did you fail on this time then?" mocked my Dad.

"Now, now Norman," said Mum, "you took four tests before you passed, remember." Good old Mum, I thought.

"Actually I passed," I announced triumphantly.

"Well, I don't believe you," said Dad. He probably did believe me but was embarrassed that he'd been unkind moments before, "let's see your pink slip then!"

I got it out of my pocket and refrained from rubbing it across his face mockingly but to his credit he took the joke well and we all had a laugh. Perhaps it was dawning on him that he now would have to give up his beloved Hillman Minx to accommodate my needs in the future!

Looking back all these year's later I must say that the driving test was the most nerve wracking experience I can recall and I was more nervous for those two tests than anything else. It seemed that so much hung on passing it not least to prevent the serious leg pulling from your mates. However, for me the change was even more significant. The test was less than three weeks after I had met Chrissie. She lived in the back of beyond and without the use of a car we could never have kept going out together. So due to my success at passing we have enjoyed nearly 40 years of happy married life together!

...

So, I could drive but had no car. I could use my Dad's at weekends but only when he was not out and about in it. As he and Mum were always out on a Saturday evening and some Sundays that became difficult but we managed to get round it so I could at least get to see Chrissie.

Not many boys had cars enabling them to drive to school. There were exceptions. Howard Swan, a good friend then and still is now, had a Mini Cooper so none of us could compete with that! Ian Gunn's Mum had an ordinary Mini but four people inside was a squeeze and he always had a girlfriend so the eight of us who often socialised together still had to make do with shank's pony or the local bus service or our thumbs for a lift.

In my final year at the school in the seventh form, where I was to re-sit my flunked A-levels from the previous year, we had an American turn up for one year at the school to prepare for and sit his A-levels with us.

None of us would have met an American before but we had a good diet of American shows on TV even then and thought we had a pretty good understanding of what Americans were like.

Gary Smith did not disappoint us and soon became one of the "lads" – he was confident, brash, cocky but a little naïve (so typically American really), yet great fun.

Now we all thought he epitomised the old wartime adage of the Americans that they were "overpaid, oversexed and over here" and Gary was a little like that. He always had loads of cash and charmed the birds out of the trees or more likely off the dance floor.

What was it that attracted these girls to a Yank, we asked? Could it be they fantasised to be with Rock Hudson (!), Steve McQueen or Paul Newman and Gary was the next best thing? For goodness sake he wore glasses! Perhaps it was due not only to the fact that he had a car that he poignantly (to us at least) managed to park right outside the school gates so we could not miss it but more annoyingly the car was a red Ford Mustang!

So throaty was its exhaust that the old school buildings almost shook to their foundations when he roared off.

So my Dad's old Hillman Minx that was over ten years old with more than a hint of rust could not match up against Swan's Mini Cooper or Smith's Mustang but it did have one all saving thing in its favour. It had a bench seat in the front!

Now, when you were courting (as it was called in those days) and wanted a bit of slap and tickle in the car you really did need to get into the back seat with your girlfriend because in the front the gap between the seats would be awkward and the (then) long gear lever and handbrake would seriously get in the way. The Minx had a steering column gear lever and handbrake just below the dashboard that you pulled out towards you.

So in order to get to know each other better it would normally have meant getting out of the car and into the back and then out again and back into the front when it was time to go home. It was an awful lot more civilised and convenient with the bench seat especially if it was freezing cold or pouring with rain outside!

...

Steve Little

The thing we all dreaded the most would be to damage our parent's car – their pride and joy. There is not one of us from that time who has not broken down (and, of course, we would get the blame for whatever the cause might have been!) or hit something whilst in their car. I was no exception but managed to get away with it, with my Dad, in particular, not ever knowing I was responsible for a couple of scrapes.

The first was when driving into our garage. We rented one in a block about a quarter of a mile from where we lived. The only thing kept in the garage was the odd can of oil and some rags and a chamois. If it was raining and the car was wet, it always had to be wiped dry before locking up to prevent more rusting! Anyway this particular dark night I opened the garage's double wooden doors and leapt into the car and swept in but got the angle wrong. The passenger side scraped along the wooden whitewashed doorframe and I reversed out horrified. The whole of that side of the car had three lines of white paint along the front and back wings and both doors!

Panicking and with more than a tremble in my legs I rubbed it all with a dry cloth. I cannot begin to say how relieved I was when the whitewash, fortunately the wood had not been glossed, came off and there remained barely a trace left. The trouble was that there was now one clean side of the car and the rest of it was dirty. So at close to midnight I had to clean the car. My Dad was most impressed by my kindness in cleaning his car (I had told him it had got dirty driving down the unmade road to Chrissie's house!). Little did he know how close I came to every teenage driver's nightmare!

The other occasion I had a little incident was when Chrissie and I had caught the bus to the pub where my parents and grandparents were enjoying a late evening sherry one Saturday. This was our third date and Chrissie stayed outside by the car, preferring not to meet my family at this early stage, whilst I went inside to get the car key. The pub was, fortunately for us, a couple of miles from her house so I dropped her off, but not before we had a kiss and a cuddle, and I went back to pick up the family.

When I returned the car park was full except for one space right under the tall pub sign. I'll reverse it in I thought. Crash! I'd hit the black painted base of the sign. No reversing lights or sensors in those days to tell me it protruded that much!

I leapt out. Damn! A dent and scratch on the chrome bumper. More panic! I decided to say nothing, as this was only a week after I had passed my test and, if Dad knew it was me, that could be curtains for the use of the car for the immediate future!

On the Sunday morning I was doing my homework and Dad was cleaning the car. I waited in trepidation for the explosion, which duly came. He stormed in to see my Mum, "Those bloody students at the pub last night must have reversed into the car and dented the bumper. If I see them again I'll give them a piece of my mind." Phew! Got away with it again! I went outside and commiserated with Dad when we inspected the dent. Being a sheet metal worker he soon had the dent out and the scratch removed and all was well with the world again.

...

Some of my friends were not so lucky! Nige Ottley did have his own car, a Morris Minor (hardly the boy racer type of car driven by some teenagers today!). Ian Brown drove around in his Mum's car, also a Morris Minor. One Saturday night both cars full of schoolmates drove to a club in Ilford some twenty miles up the A12 from Chelmsford.

This would normally have involved drinking but Nige was a bit under the weather and was on antibiotics so stuck to orange juice.

Typically on the way back the drivers were stretching the speed of the dependable Morris Minors to the limit and racing, if that is not being a little generous in describing what these cars were actually capable of!

The totally sober Nige, following the slightly less sober Ian, (he was still well inside the then more generous drink drive laws however!) got a bit close to Ian's bumper and as Ian slowed Nige didn't and went into the back of Mrs Brown's pride and joy.

Cue apologies and then panic at what they should tell their Mums. Unlike in my case, there was no way the damage could be corrected right away or even ignored. Bearing in mind Nige's car had cost the princely sum of £76 and no doubt Ian's would have been about the same, they could have been write-offs. Mrs Ottley to her credit paid to have the damage repaired and despite a ticking off from both Mums each chap became a better driver as a result, at least according to them!

...

So whilst this was hardly the age of the car we had great fun with them whether they were the then upmarket Mini Cooper, a Ford Mustang or just the plain old Morris Minor and Hillman Minx!

35

SOMETHING IN THE AIR

Thunderclap Newman had a massive Number One with "Something in the Air" the year after I left KEGS and whenever I hear the song now I always recall those poignant smells from the school during my time there.

Schools, even today, have many sights and sounds no different from those days in the 1960s. The noisy chatter, the shout of the teacher to walk not run, the untidy look of the teenage pupils and so on. In the 60s it was the tie askew and the cap on the back of the head, even when you are 15 and have an unruly mop in the style of Reg Presley of the Troggs. Today it is shorter hair often with large amounts of gel; then there are the designer trainers and the obligatory shirt outside of the trousers for the boys.

Also, there is the smell of schools. They do not change much either. I have frequently visited the school where my daughter teaches as I have

Days We'll Remember All Our Lives

coached football to the after-school club and look after the school team. Any time I go into the school there is always the whiff of disinfectant, the smell of new gloss paint particularly prevalent in September and then the slight smell of used shoes and children's sweaty feet.

In the 1960s the same smells prevailed.

- The main building at KEGS was built in the 1890s and would not have had radiators in the rooms at first but these were subsequently added and they were of the old metal ringed design with thermostats that did not turn, having seized up years before. The joints had been glossed so many times the nuts were set solid. Like every other school some of the radiators would get a summer holiday coat of paint and by the first week of September, when we went back, there was the smell of white gloss almost all round the school, especially as those classrooms containing the newly painted radiator would have had their doors closed and windows shut during the warmth of July and August to build up the smell. As we began to get used to the smell, October 1st came round and whether or not it was the start of winter (invariably though we were enjoying an Indian summer) the heating was turned on. Unable to adjust the thermostat the classrooms resembled the tropics and with many masters not allowing us to remove our jackets, sweaty smells prevailed and it was particularly unpleasant for the next class using that room to face the awful smell. Sometimes the new class waited outside for the smell to drift out into the corridor before they felt it safe to go inside.

- The odour of disinfectant was constant. No doubt it was used to wipe over the floor of the hall, library, gym and changing rooms and even the classrooms at times but an overriding memory of the smell is associated with someone being sick. It happened from time to time. Once, notably, poor old Forster from our year was sick in Assembly when it was held in the old Hall. He had not felt it coming and did not make for the exit. I can recall the sound of the splash on the floor even now! We were in the third year and that morning we had to go back to the Hall for a talk by "Brom" Bromwich, one of the senior masters, about our subject choices for the next year ahead of our O-level syllabus. Not being very good with "sick" I entered the Hall in trepidation as I recalled the smell from earlier of Forster's regurgitated bacon and egg! The only smell was the disinfectant but that just reminded me of the smell of the sick and it was making me feel ill. "Brom" saved the day for me. He had a pipe and filled it with his favoured St. Bruno and I sat back in my chair as this lovely, sweet smell wafted over me. It was like nectar to me.

- I was never good at all with people being ill like this. As I have already mentioned earlier, I sat next to Ian Brown once on the coach back from Wales and he had had too much to drink the night before, eaten a far too rich "Full Welsh" and he only lasted a few miles on the coach before he had to hastily get off. No problem with that but when he returned to his seat, which just happened to be next to me, he smelt of sick and I had to endure the smell for another four hours – he was fine but it made me feel queasy!

- Another coach trip and another incident. Clive Haworth was a travel sickness sufferer (so why did he opt to go on coach trips I always asked myself!) and we were off to the White City to watch the international athletics. He had to sit in the front of the coach with Mr Elder the teacher and had a newspaper fitted into the gap between his legs into which he could be sick as necessary. No more than two miles along the road we went over a humped back bridge and he was off! Cue usual unpleasant smell and me feeling queasy for the rest of the journey!

- Nearly 50 years later certain other smells are remembered more fondly. Although Woodwork lessons themselves were never fondly recalled, the smell of sawn or planed wood had that soothing, satisfying aroma that mystically drew us into the workshop to the hell that was trying to make a wooden box with dovetail joints and a lid to the satisfaction of Mr Danvers!

- Mown grass was a sign of the spring and summer. The school had two quadrangles with a rectangular lawn in the middle and mown neatly into strips once April came around. It masked the disinfectant and made you want to dash to the sports shed and get the cricket gear out!

- Despite these more pleasant memories there were some others that were less so. Until the new gym was built the old one had two changing rooms and each had its own shower with about six showerheads in each. After Games lessons up to a hundred boys from one year would crowd into these two rooms. All sweaty and muddy. The showers, when occasionally hot, would belch out steam which when mixed with the odour from the boys' exertions on the sports field created a unique scent! The showers were in constant use and not having any suitable ventilation they added that acute damp smell to that delicious scent in the rest of the changing room. We should have bottled it up and called it "Sport D'Homme" or something similar!

- Individual body odour in a school of over 600 boys would always be an issue. Generally it was not too bad (but perhaps we all smelt a bit!) but there were exceptions. One boy in our year was a case in point. He was always sweaty looking. His skin was more reddish than looked healthy and maybe it was a medical condition – none of us knew. But if you touched his hands they were extremely sweaty, even wet. We all avoided sitting next to him as he had that smell of rotting fruit. It was better than the onion smell of some but was still unpleasant. One can only wonder what his parents did to help and how he turned out later in life and whether he wooed someone to share his life! We did not help with any subtle guidance as he was nicknamed "Smelly" – but normally behind his back!

- The masters never had any such personal problems. We had an East African Indian who taught Maths and he had a different but not unpleasant smell about him. We put that down to his diet because we had read somewhere that we western Europeans would smell pretty revolting to him because of our diet of red meat and that this was particularly noticeable to the Africans. It seemed plausible enough! "Bruiser" Findlay, the fearsome Deputy Head, would often visit the "Compasses" at lunchtime and sit in the corner avoiding the gaze of the group of sixth formers enjoying a pint at the bar. He liked his Scotch and if you had Maths in the afternoon with him and he leant over you to explain Pythagoras there was the unmistakable smell on his breath of Whyte & Mackay.

- Although as one pupil who never had school dinners, I could not but avoid the smell of Mrs Springett's cooking. With 600 mouths to feed in two sittings that was a lot of cabbage and tapioca. The cooking smell of vegetables permeated the whole school during the morning and was not always appetising. Although chips were not often on the menu the smell of them permanently existed in and around the refectory as the school liked to call it – dinner hall to most of us. So as we passed by it on the way to morning assembly there always seemed to be the aroma of yesterday's chips!

- Another anathema to me was milk. Pre Margaret Thatcher we had our daily ration in school of a third of a pint but I never indulged and traded mine for an iced bun from the tuck shop. The smell of milk turns my stomach even now especially if it is creamy. I can take it in tea and coffee but straight from the bottle? – No thanks! Anyway I managed to get by without it but with my mates enjoying theirs (and mine!) I had to endure THAT smell and it always turned my stomach. In class immediately after the morning break I might have to sit next to a boy that had enjoyed his daily dose. I could always smell the milk on his clothes and his breath. It always made me gag.

So nearly 50 years on some of the smells remain. That of cabbage is rare these days, which can only be a good thing and Mrs Thatcher the Snatcher got rid of the milk, to me a far more significant event than saving the Falklands!

With the teenagers today masking their natural smells with aftershave even though they rarely shave and putting copious amounts of gel on their hair, it means that some of the general school aroma is pleasant. Woodwork rooms (Thank God!) have gone. Teachers never drink at lunchtimes. So, "the times they are a-changin'" as Bob Dylan once said but the disinfectant, the paint and the feet? Still there I'm afraid!

36

THE END OF THOSE DAYS

So by the summer of 1968 those days at KEGS came to an end and poignantly and most appropriately Mary Hopkin was to top the Charts with "Those were the days" some of the lyrics of which are as follows: -

Those were the days my friend
We thought they'd never end
We'd sing and dance forever and a day
We'd live the life we choose
We'd fight and never lose
For we were young and sure to have our way.
Those were the days, oh yes those were the days

(Lyrics by Gene Raskin)

For some it was off to university for others it was work. Most of my friends had left in 1967 but some stayed on in the seventh form as we chose to re-sit our A-levels and then try for university. Still at the end of it some of us still decided to avoid university and seek our way in the world.

Days We'll Remember All Our Lives

What a change from 1960 to 1968. Looking back now the social revolution that took place in those few years rivalled any in history as the country moved from post war austerity to the beginning of the modern era. Music had changed the world. Fashion had gone from collar and tie and flowing frocks to kaftans, flares and mini-skirts. The permissive society had begun with the widespread use of the contraceptive pill. Capital punishment had gone. Men were looking to land on the Moon. England had won the World Cup thanks to some help from a Russian linesman, who in an instant perhaps remembered what the Germans had done to some of his family!

If we'd never had it so good in 1960, according to our then Prime Minister, we had it even better by 1968. So, indeed looking back they were the "Days We'll Remember All Our Lives" – those boys at KEGS who stood in that playground in straggly lines waiting to be placed in Form 1A, 1B or 1C are now over 50 years older. Some are now grandfathers, many are retired after careers as diverse as one could imagine but some, sadly, have passed away. We remember them as we remember those days so succinctly described by Ray Davies of the Kinks when he wrote about "Days" in 1968: -

Steve Little

Thank you for the days,
Those endless days, those sacred days you gave me.
I'm thinking of the days,
I won't forget a single day, believe me.

I bless the light,
I bless the light that lights on you believe me.
And though you're gone,
You're with me every single day, believe me.

Days I'll remember all my life,
Days when you can't see wrong from right.
You took my life,
But then I knew that very soon you'd leave me,
But it's all right,
Now I'm not frightened of this world, believe me.

I wish today could be tomorrow,
The night is dark,
It just brings sorrow anyway.

Thank you for the days.